W9-BGT-523

"David Rome has mastered Focusing, a method for using the body's wisdom to navigate life's major decisions. *Your Body Knows the Answer* makes this invaluable tool available to us all."

—DANIEL GOLEMAN, author of *Emotional Intelligence* and *Focus*

"Reading David Rome's book opened a forgotten but familiar doorway in my heart that sang, 'yes!' He returns us to our bodies, showing us how to access the felt sense, the nonconceptual experience of embodied knowing we have been yearning for. He skillfully guides us to wholeness, introducing accessible exercises that form a toolkit for life. Mindful Focusing comes at a perfect time, resting at the nexus of mindfulness, neuroscience, and social-emotional learning, showing the way for us to bridge meditation and daily life, the brain and the heart, Western philosophy and Eastern wisdom. This book is a treasure to savor—and use—again and again."

—ACHARYA JUDITH SIMMER-BROWN, Distinguished Professor of Contemplative and Religious Studies, Naropa University, and author of *Dakini's Warm Breath: The Feminine Principle in Tibetan Buddhism*

Your Body Knows
the Answer

Using Your Felt Sense to Solve Problems,
Effect Change, and Liberate Creativity

DAVID I. ROME

SHAMBHALA
Boston & London
2014

Shambhala Publications, Inc.
Horticultural Hall
300 Massachusetts Avenue
Boston, Massachusetts 02115
www.shambhala.com

© 2014 by David I. Rome

All rights reserved. No part of this book may be
reproduced in any form or by any means, electronic
or mechanical, including photocopying, recording,
or by any information storage and retrieval system,
without permission in writing from the publisher.

9 8 7 6 5 4 3 2 1

First Edition
Printed in the United States of America

♾ This edition is printed on acid-free paper that meets the
American National Standards Institute z39.48 Standard.
♻ This book was printed on 30% post-consumer recycled paper.
For more information please visit www.shambhala.com.

Distributed in the United States by Penguin Random House LLC
and in Canada by Random House of Canada Ltd

Library of Congress Cataloging-in-Publication Data
Rome, David I.
Your body knows the answer: using your felt sense to solve
problems, effect change, and liberate creativity / David I. Rome.
pages cm
ISBN 978-1-61180-090-6 (pbk.)
1. Mind and body. 2. Buddhism. I. Title.
BF161.R753 2014
294.3'361537—dc23
2013050190

To the memory of my parents,
CHAWA AND HERZL,
who loved me into existence.

Contents

Preface

I N THE SUMMER OF 1971, shortly after I returned to New York from two eye-opening years as a Peace Corps volunteer in Kenya, my high-school friend Alex invited me to bum around Europe for a couple of months. Starting in England, we took in the primordial megaliths of Stonehenge, the soaring cathedral at Salisbury, the legendary Glastonbury Tor where King Arthur came in search of the Holy Grail. I was duly impressed by these sights, yet they had the curious effect of making me feel lost, un-moored, empty. I couldn't connect my own existence to these marvels. For that matter, I couldn't really seem to connect with anything in the world around me at this time.

Alex, a Gandhian political activist, had recently spent time in India and as our next destination had his heart set on a "Tibetan monastery" in Scotland. With little enthusiasm, I accompanied him on the long drive to a barren, windswept countryside where a former hunting lodge was now in use as a Buddhist meditation center. Feeling even more out of my element than before in this odd place, but also intrigued, I dutifully sat on a low cushion, joined in the strange chanting as best I could, and followed the simple instructions for silent meditation. As I sat there uncom-fortably, and the minutes grew longer and longer, almost im-perceptibly at first I began to touch something new in myself. There was no flash of light, no altered state of consciousness, but a different quality of awareness was dawning in me. I had no words for it, but knew I was experiencing something that had a rightness or realness, an actuality, that had been missing from my life.

Samye Ling was the name of the meditation center, and it included a small bookstore with a selection of the few books in English on Buddhism available at that time. One in particular caught my eye, a slender volume called *Meditation in Action* by Chögyam Trungpa Rinpoche, the young Tibetan lama who had started the center a few years earlier and who, I learned, was now living and teaching in North America. I read the little book on the plane returning to the States, and in October, that magical month when New England is aflame with multihued foliage and bright blue sky, I drove to northern Vermont to visit Tail of the Tiger (now called Karmê Chöling), the new meditation center established by Trungpa Rinpoche's first American students. There I met my teacher, collected windfall apples and pressed them into fragrant cider, and began in earnest a lifelong study and practice of Buddhism.

The next summer, I moved to Boulder, Colorado, the old mining town and seat of the University of Colorado at the foot of the Rocky Mountains that Trungpa Rinpoche had made his new home and headquarters. In January 1974, after participating in Rinpoche's first annual three-month advanced-teaching Seminary, I had the good fortune to become his private secretary, a role in which I served for more than nine years. This period marked the flood tide of Trungpa Rinpoche's extraordinarily diverse creative contributions—including the founding of the Naropa Institute (now Naropa University) that summer—which have had such a profound effect on the development of Western Buddhism and contemporary contemplative practice in general.

These were also years of significant personal growth for me. I met and married my wife, Martha, our daughter Rebecca was born, and I made fast friendships that endure to this day. We left Boulder in 1983 to live in New York City, where I went to work at Schocken Books, the small but distinguished publishing company founded by my grandfather Salman Schocken. During this time I edited books, found and renovated new offices for the firm, and learned much about the challenges of the for-profit business world, including serving as president of the company for two years before its sale to Random House in 1987. There followed six years in Halifax, Nova Scotia, Trungpa Rinpoche's new seat and today the headquarters of Shambhala International, the worldwide network of meditation centers under the guidance of Trungpa's son Sakyong Mipham Rinpoche.

In 1993, I accepted an invitation from the pioneering Buddhist social activist Bernie Glassman, a Jewish-American Zen roshi, to join the Greyston Foundation, a mandala of for-profit and non-profit organizations in Yonkers, New York, devoted to inner-city community development and human services. This was a refreshing return to the kind of service that had begun during my Peace Corps years in East Africa, now blended with my Buddhist contemplative path. The twelve years I spent at Greyston were a time of real fulfillment—yet somewhere in me, at a level I was only fitfully aware of, a sense of something missing was stirring, not unlike what I had experienced in my twenties. I wanted deeper access to my own feelings. Also, at this time I experienced my first serious, prolonged illness.

While browsing one day in a rural Vermont used bookstore, I happened upon a little mass-market paperback. Filling its entire cover was a slightly abstract photograph of stones of different colors, shapes, and sizes, seen through the surface of a gently rippling stream. The title was a single word: *Focusing*. The name of the author, Eugene Gendlin, was unfamiliar. Curious, I paid two-and-a-half dollars for the small volume.

As *Meditation in Action* had done years earlier, *Focusing* opened up for me a whole new territory of self-understanding. While mindfulness-awareness practice had illuminated many mental, physical, and emotional subtleties in my life I might not otherwise have recognized, core aspects of my makeup remained hidden. Meditation is wonderful for stepping away from the speed and complexities of everyday life and finding refuge in a calmer, more spacious quality of mind, but it can be insufficient to bring to light the deeper roots of feeling, memory, and belief, including sources of emotional and creative blockage. Also, given its emphasis on "bare attention"—merely noting what arises in present-moment experience, then letting it go—it is not the best tool for practical problem solving (the Buddha, after all, was a monk who renounced worldly life in order to penetrate to the root of human suffering and realize the ultimate nature of reality). The technique that Eugene Gendlin named Focusing supplied the link that had been missing for me: a simple but powerful means to bridge from sitting meditation practice to the nitty-gritty of everyday life. It was a contemplative method for uncovering and working with my deeper feelings and solving the specific, real-life challenges of work, marriage, parenting, and much more.

Mindful Focusing, the method for problem-solving and inner cultivation introduced in this book, reflects the personal journey I have described. I offer it as a new integration of a powerful introspective technique from modern Western philosophy and psychology with ancient mindfulness-awareness practices that originated in India three millennia ago.

I am profoundly indebted to the extraordinary teachers I have had the privilege to learn from and be guided by, first and foremost Chögyam Trungpa Rinpoche and Eugene Gendlin. The seismic contributions of these two geniuses of the human experience are central to this book. Other thought leaders and cultural creatives who have influenced my work and provided personal guidance for which I am deeply grateful include Ashley Bryan, Allen Ginsberg, Arawana Hayashi, Robert Kegan, Otto Scharmer, Peter Senge, Daniel Siegel, and Francisco Varela.

I have been deeply influenced by the life-nourishing body-awareness work of Hope Martin, master practitioner of the Alexander Technique, who has been my personal teacher as well as my cocreator and teaching partner in the Embodied Listening program. My understanding of Focusing has been nurtured and shaped by master teachers Ann Weiser Cornell, Mary Hendricks Gendlin, Robert Lee, Kye Nelson, and my dear friend and Focusing partner Carolyn Worthing.

My heart holds a special place for the people and places that have sponsored, hosted, and published my work: Michael Chender and Susan Szpakowski at ALIA; Melinda Darer at the Focusing Institute; Diana Rose, Rob Gabriele, Tish Jennings, and Mary Pearl at the Garrison Institute; Julie Martin at Goddard College; Bernie and Jishu Glassman and Charles Lief at the Greyston Foundation; Patton Hyman at Karmê Chöling; Richard Brown, Susan Skjei, Mark Wilding, and Charles Lief (again) at Naropa University; Jim Kullander at Omega Institute; Tracy Cochran at *Parabola;* Dale Asrael, Adam Lobel, and other individuals too numerous to list at Shambhala International centers throughout North America and in Europe; Melvin McLeod, James Gimian, and Barry Boyce at the *Shambhala Sun* and *Mindful* magazine; Craig Richards, Robin Stern, and Aliki Nicolaides at Teachers College, Columbia University; Andrew Cooper and Sam Mowe at *Tricycle;* and Jim and Margaret Drescher at Windhorse Farm.

For encouragement, guidance, and support both practical and emotional, thank you Michael Baime, David Bolduc, Richard Brown, Michael Carroll, Gayna Havens, Evan Henritze, Carol Hyman, Roger and Susan Lipsey, Andy and Wendy Karr, Jackie Meuse, Susan Piver, Dan Rome, Rebecca Rome, Jim Rosen, David Sable, Rose Sposito, and so many more colleagues, friends, and family.

I am keenly indebted to a generous cohort of readers whose discerning comments at different stages of writing have rescued me from various faux pas and infelicities (while leaving me accountable for those that remain): Barbara Bash, Ann Weiser Cornell, Joan Klagsbrun, Ellen Meisels, Jerome Murphy, Martha Rome, Pamela Seigle, Donna Siegel, and Rona Wilensky.

Editor Dave O'Neal and his wonderfully talented and dedicated colleagues at Shambhala Publications have been both a privilege and a pleasure to work with, as has copy editor *extraordinaire* Tracy Davis.

This book would not exist were it not for F. Joseph Spieler, dear friend of many decades and my agent, whose admonishments over the years—"You have a book in you"; "Write what you know"—gave me the confidence to attempt it in the first place, and whose sage counsel and unfaltering faith guided it to fruition. Joe, I owe you more than words can express.

Finally, neither this book nor I as the person capable of writing it would exist without the love, loyalty, discernment, patience, impatience, and deeply nurturing companionship of my wife of thirty-seven years. Thank you, Martha, for making it all possible.

Your Body Knows the Answer

Introduction

WHAT DO THE FOLLOWING situations have in common?

- You know there's more to life, but you don't know how to find it.
- You have trouble getting in touch with your feelings.
- You experience intense emotions that are painful to you and sometimes get you in trouble with other people.
- Your work is not fulfilling.
- You're in too many fights with your partner, or with a family member, work colleague, or friend.
- You know what you have to do but can't get yourself started.
- You experience sudden, critical thoughts about your own intelligence, appearance, or ability.
- You have a decision to make and keep going through the pluses and minuses, but still aren't sure what to do.
- Something feels off, but you can't identify what it is.
- You've made a good start on a creative project, but now you're stuck and nothing you do feels right.
- There are things about yourself you'd like to change, but you don't know how.

It is easy enough to recognize that all these situations involve some kind of personal challenge. Some of them are clearly problems; others are more like opportunities. Or, as is so often the case, they are problems that also provide opportunities, or opportunities that also present problems. Their common denominator is that all of them require *change*. Further, the change they require is not straightforward and simple like changing the tires on your car when they wear out, nor is it even a big, complicated kind of change like moving to a different part of the country for a new job or school.

The kind of change all of these situations call for, be they large or small, is an *inner* change. They require a kind of change whose steps are not at all obvious at first and that, although other people may give you helpful advice and information, ultimately no one can take but you. Inner change of the kind I'm talking about calls upon you to *do something you don't know how to do.*

Mindful Focusing is a learnable inner skill involving mind, body, and heart that will show you a different way of working with precisely those problems that seem to have no answers.

The Neuroscience of a Balanced Life

As the new field of cognitive neuroscience illuminates more and more about the complex workings of the human brain, we are coming to appreciate the brain as the supreme organ of coordination, integration, and balancing of life processes. Recent research has focused on differences in the function of the brain's right and left hemispheres. Whereas the left brain specializes in language, logic, repetitive patterns, and control mechanisms, the right brain oversees body awareness, emotions, creativity, and resilience in the face of novel situations. Modern culture has increasingly emphasized the left-brain functions and neglected right-brain capacities. (The disappearance of art and music from many public-school curricula is one disturbing example.)

We have reached a point in our evolution as a species where this accelerating overspecialization in language and logical thought, and the immensely powerful technologies and ecological turbulence that it has spawned, endanger our survival. There is a loss of balance and wholeness in individual lives and in our shared life as a society. Not only our mental health but our sense of meaning, identity, and purpose—not to mention happiness—depends on bringing the diverse life-enhancing functions of our brains back into balance. This book presents Mindful Focusing, a unique synthesis of two mind-body disciplines, one ancient and one modern, that is a highly effective means for cultivating balance, good health, enjoyment, accomplishment, and wisdom in our lives.

The ancient practice of mindfulness cultivates calmness, clarity, and emotional balance through sustained attention to present-moment experience. Cognitive neuroscience, by means of powerful new technologies like functional magnetic resonance imaging (fMRI), is validating the multiple physiological as well as psychological benefits of mindfulness techniques, including stress reduction, cardiovascular health, improved mood, and increased emotional intelligence. Chögyam Trungpa Rinpoche described mindfulness practice simply as a way of making friends with yourself.

Focusing is a modern mind-body awareness method whose efficacy in reducing stress, improving resilience, and fostering personal growth is also demonstrated by a growing body of research. In recent years, Focusing has expanded from its origins in psychotherapy to numerous practical applications in fields ranging from education to medicine to business. Chapters 10 and 11 give more background about both mindfulness and Focusing. Right now I want to focus on the breakthrough discovery that lies at the heart of Mindful Focusing.

Finding the Felt Sense

In the 1950s, Eugene Gendlin, a young graduate student at the University of Chicago working with the great American psychologist Carl Rogers, set out to discover why some people in therapy have successful outcomes and others don't. Through carefully controlled analysis of scores of audiotaped psychotherapy sessions, Gendlin and his team were able to demonstrate that the crucial variable was not the kind of therapy practiced or even the skill of the therapist but rather a capacity that the successful clients manifested from the very first session that the unsuccessful clients lacked. This was the ability to connect with and speak from a *nonconceptual, bodily felt experience* of the issues that were troubling them.

Instead of speaking in fully formed, logically consistent sentences, the successful clients expressed themselves in a more tentative, uncertain, groping manner. They might tell the therapist, "I'm not sure how to say this." Or they might say one thing, then stop and say it differently: "I have this kind of heavy feeling in my chest; well, not exactly heavy, it's more like oppressive . . ." By analyzing the speech patterns of the successful clients—those who were able to get fresh insights into their problems and actually make positive steps of change—Gendlin demonstrated that these individuals were in touch with some kind of unclear inner sensation, a bodily felt *meaning* that couldn't be fully expressed in words. Gendlin called this nonverbal inner source of knowing the bodily felt sense, or simply the felt sense.

Felt senses can be found in a subtle, mostly unrecognized zone of experiencing inside us, a kind of border zone between our conscious and unconscious. This level of experience lies below our everyday awareness of objects, thoughts, emotions, and beliefs. It is an embryonic form of awareness in which "body" and "mind" are not separate. Felt senses are both *bodily experienced* and *meaningful*. They *embody* the unique reality of our individual lives in ways that can't yet be put into words.

Felt senses are unclear somatic sensations that for the most part go unnoticed, yet they are not wholly unconscious. They can be "found" by bringing a special quality of gentle mindfulness to the zone of subtle bodily experiencing in which they form. When attended to with friendly but dispassionate attention, felt senses that start out vague and indescribable can show up with greater clarity and presence. A felt sense can come alive and offer what it already knows about life situations that you—the conscious, conceptualizing you—don't yet know. Entering into a process of inquiry with the felt sense invites spontaneous flashes of intuitive insight that generate novel perceptions and understandings, leading to fresh solutions to life's challenges.

When the conceptual mind loses its moment-to-moment connection to direct bodily experience, it begins to take on a life of its own. Conceptual mind is very good at identifying parts and putting different parts together in new combinations, but it is not good at holding a sense of the whole. It can lose touch with the reality of our lives, creating alternative realities, both pleasant and unpleasant, that are inaccurate or incomplete.

Of course, there are times when this ability of the human conceptual mind to think abstractly—that is, abstracted from bodily experiencing—is highly useful. We can feel that $2 + 2 = 4$ is true and $2 + 2 = 5$ is false, but most of us can't "feel" that $2365 + 3472 = 5837$ without going through the logical steps of checking the addition. Modern science and technology and much else depends on such abstract thinking, but in our daily lives far too often our conceptual minds create constructs—ideas built with words—that are disconnected from our lived reality. This is a source of great frustration and suffering.

Accessing the body's more holistic knowing can bring us back into accurate relationship with our life situations. This often involves acknowledging aspects of our lives that are not as we would like them to be, or as we would like others to see us. But knowing ourselves as we really are, and seeing things as they really are, provides the only basis for a wholesome, genuine, and truly productive life. "Know thyself," the ancient Greeks taught. Gendlin's mentor Carl Rogers said, "The curious paradox is that when I accept myself as I am, then I can change."[1]

Finding the felt sense is a powerful way of knowing yourself deeply, accepting yourself as you truly are in the present moment, and also changing yourself in directions that are genuinely life enhancing.

How Will Finding Your Felt Sense Benefit You?

The felt sense is a place of hidden treasures that each of us carries inside ourselves. The purpose of this book is to give you some tools with which you can begin to unearth that treasure. Finding the felt sense allows us to bring a deeper kind of knowing to life situations, problems, decisions, and creative challenges. This deeper knowing can then lead to insights and action steps to shift aspects of our life that feel stuck, releasing fresh energy and bringing welcome forward movement to our lives.

If you have trouble accessing your feelings, Mindful Focusing can provide a key to open the lockers in which they are hidden. That is exactly what first brought me to the practice of finding the felt sense. On the other hand, if you are dealing with too much emotion, Mindful Focusing can show you how not to become overwhelmed or paralyzed by powerful feelings. It is a gradual process of developing a trusting relationship with all the different parts of yourself, including aspects of your experience that it hasn't been safe to bring into consciousness. Felt-sensing gives us a way to acknowledge and change things that have been holding us back rather than falling victim to them.

Finding the felt sense also brings profound benefits to our

relationships with others. Instead of reacting from momentary thoughts and emotions, we develop the mental, psychological, and emotional space to respond from a deeper and wiser place in ourselves. Drawing on the felt sense changes how we listen and speak, how we learn and think, how we decide and create. It has the power to make us more resilient, more insightful, and more productive, as well as both more autonomous in ourselves and better partners with others. It also makes a wonderful complement to other methods for personal growth and healthy living, including exercise and bodywork, psychotherapy, meditation, and spiritual practices.

You may be wondering, if finding the felt sense is so versatile and effective, why is this technique not more widely known? There are several answers. Finding and working with the felt sense is not flashy and is not a quick fix; it takes time and commitment to learn; it can and will bring you up against uncomfortable places in yourself; last, but not least, it goes against the grain of our contemporary culture with its emphasis on speed and instant gratification and its information overload, digital social networking, obsession with appearances, materialism, and endless varieties of egoism.

Human beings are like icebergs: much of who we really are and what motivates our behavior lies below the level of ordinary consciousness. By learning how to access our innate but neglected capacity for bodily knowing, we can bring to light lost or alienated parts of ourselves and discover how to meet the unmet needs that they embody. Then these parts can reintegrate and contribute to positive change, growth, and fulfillment.

How to Use This Book

Once you are proficient in finding the felt sense, you'll be able to do it almost anywhere and anytime—in the elevator before an important meeting, during the meeting itself, while walking, while driving. But to learn and then deepen your felt-sensing skills, you will need to devote some deliberate time and energy.

Each person's learning journey is unique. Some are able to locate felt senses quickly, while for many it will take repeated attempts. If you find you are in the latter category, don't be discouraged. Even if you find nothing at first, the basic practice described in chapter 1 of bringing open, friendly awareness to what's going on inside your body will stimulate felt senses to show up after a while. Think of it like spring seeds planted in the earth— for a while you don't see anything coming up, but you have to keep watering!

It is also important to know in advance that the process of finding the felt sense can be uncomfortable. You will be entering unfamiliar inner territory, and you are likely to encounter places that are strange, scary, painful, or disorienting. Your reward for staying on the path even when it's uncomfortable will be arriving at new places that have a wonderful feeling of rightness, insight, and freedom.

This book is divided into two parts. Part 1 focuses on the theme of making friends with yourself or, as the section title says, making friends *in* yourself. It presents a step-by-step introduction to the practice of Mindful Focusing. Each chapter includes one or more exercises designed to elicit specific inner skills that, taken together, constitute a toolkit or repertoire you can draw on as you deepen your practice and start to apply it to many different kinds of challenges.

Part 2, "Living Life Forward," goes into greater detail on applying Mindful Focusing in specific contexts. It begins with the challenge of converting insights into actions, then looks at how to draw on felt senses to meet challenges in relationships, communication, conflict situations, and decision making. After that it considers how Mindful Focusing deepens intellectual understanding and aesthetic discernment, its role in creative process, and how it increases awareness and appreciation of nature and the environment. The concluding chapter explores the vital role of felt-sensing in the spiritual dimension of our lives. As in part 1, each chapter contains one or more exercises you can do on your own or, in some cases, with others.

Between parts 1 and 2, there is a two-chapter interlude that goes into greater depth about the two principal traditions that come together in Mindful Focusing: ancient Buddhist mindfulness-awareness meditation practices and Eugene Gendlin's contemporary Philosophy of the Implicit, a radically new understanding of the nature of living things and life process that underlies his discovery and development of Focusing. If sources and theory are important in your way of learning, you're welcome to read the interlude at any point. If theory isn't your cup of tea, you can skip it altogether.

The exercises are the heart of the book. You can get some insight from just reading the text, but finding the felt sense is fundamentally about getting in touch with our preconceptual nature, and it is through doing the exercises that you will discover your own unique way of doing that. The exercises in part 1 are foundational. I recommend reading a chapter at a time and repeating the exercises several times before going on to the next chapter. You will progress most rapidly if you set aside time every day to work on these practices. As with any new skill, repetition will lead to mastery.

If a particular exercise doesn't seem to be working for you after several repetitions, give it a break and move on to the next. You can return to the problem exercise later on and see if it is more fruitful. In fact, it will be helpful to repeat earlier exercises at any point. As your felt-sensing ability improves with practice, you will continue to make new discoveries.

One of my favorite records when I was growing up was *Bert and I*, a collection of Down East New England humor. In one story, a motorist stops to ask a local for directions to Millinocket, a remote town in northern Maine. The local scratches his head and then says, "Now, if you stay on this road another three blocks, then turn right at the filling station and get on the big highway, and stay on that all the way to . . ." and then he trails off. "Well, no," he continues, "you better keep going on this road for another seven miles till you see the general store on your left, then . . ." and again he trails off. He tries a third time, "Actually, the thing to do is get on the coastal route all the tourists take and follow that right along until . . ." Finally, after a long pause, he announces, "Come to think of it—you can't get there from here!"

This book is about the kinds of challenges that feel like "you can't get there from here." It is about a whole different way of meeting challenges and making change. I have experienced in my own life, and seen over and over in the lives of others, how truly life changing these practices can be. I hope you will experience similar insight and transformation as you explore the hidden riches of your own felt sense.

Part One

Making Friends
in Yourself

Chapter *1*

Steps toward Finding
the Felt Sense

IN THE COURSE of a long letter written in 1817 to his brothers in America, the English poet John Keats described a sudden realization he had while walking home from the theater with a friend:

> . . . several things dovetailed in my mind, & at once it struck me, what quality went to form a Man of Achievement, especially in Literature & which Shakespeare possessed so enormously—I mean *Negative Capability*, that is when man is capable of being in uncertainties, Mysteries, doubts, without any irritable reaching after fact & reason.[1]

This brief passage has become famous for defining the concept of negative capability. In calling it negative, Keats does not mean it is undesirable. On the contrary, this capacity is highly positive for those who possess it. Keats means negative in the sense of being empty of specific content, uncertain, unclear. He is pointing to a creative mental state of *not knowing* that is able to remain calm and open without an "irritable reaching after fact and reason."

Negative capability is crucial to the creative process of artists. It is equally important in contemplative practices like meditation and finding the felt sense. True contemplation, as opposed to ordinary discursive thinking and rumination, involves what biologist and cognitive neuroscientist Francisco Varela called a "reversal of attention." One suspends one's habitual flow of thought and feeling so as to make room for *a different way of paying attention.*

To say this more simply, Mindful Focusing begins with creating a gap in our habitual patterns of physical, psychological, and mental activity. This gap is empty of specific content, yet not empty of awareness. It is simply awareness itself—open and receptive, conscious without needing any object to be conscious of. It is a state of grounded, aware presence.

The first exercise is called GAP, both because it is about creating this particular type of gap in our consciousness and because the acronym *GAP* can stand for the state of grounded aware presence.

Exercise 1.1   GAP: Grounded Aware Presence

You may want to start by stretching your limbs, wiggling your toes, even loosening up your whole body with a refreshing shake-out. Then, find a comfortable seated position and simply become aware of your body. Sense its position, weight, and inner space.

After a while, center your attention at your base, your seat, where your body is supported by whatever you are sitting on. Feel the weight of your whole body and how it is planted on the earth. Trusting yourself to the earth's solidity, let your body really settle and be at ease. Appreciate the simplicity of being bodily present, here and now. Say the word *grounded* softly to yourself.

Next, bring your attention to the head region. Close your eyes, or lower your gaze. Concentrate your awareness on your sense of hearing. Be open and sensitive to any sound from the environment, especially the kinds of background noise that we usually don't notice at all. You can note sounds with a simple mental label—*bird singing, traffic noise, refrigerator hum*—but try not to enter into a discursive thought process. At the same time, try to notice the larger quality of silence that surrounds whatever you hear from moment to moment. Sense the whole space around you, extending even beyond the walls and what you can see from where you sit. Experience the vast, panoramic quality of awareness. Say to yourself softly *aware*.

Now move your attention into the center of your chest, place your hand gently over your heart, and experience the quality of presence. You are simply here, alive, breathing, feeling, experiencing your basic existence. It is happening right now, at this very moment. Softly repeat the word *present*.

Finally, let your attention encompass your whole body and repeat to yourself, *grounded aware presence*. Rest there for a few seconds. Then, gently open your eyes, raise your gaze, and extend your grounded aware presence to include the environment around you.

In addition to being the preparatory step in finding the felt sense, this gap, or state of grounded aware presence, is a place we can always return to in ourselves. Think of it as a trustworthy, neutral home base you can come back to any time you feel out of balance, preoccupied, or confused. You can also do the GAP exercise while standing: start by placing your attention on your feet instead of your seat, then move to your head and heart in turn, reminding yourself with the words *grounded, aware,* and *present*.

Friendly Attending

By generating grounded aware presence, we create an open space, a kind of positive emptiness that can accommodate fresh experiences. It is like clearing your desk of accumulated papers and knickknacks so that you have a clean space for work. After this preparation is done, you can begin the actual process of finding the felt sense.

The next step is to focus our *intention* and *attention* in a particular way. This is somewhat like adjusting the resolution on a microscope so that you can bring into focus the particular area you are interested in exploring. We need to resolve our *intention* to an attitude of sincere empathy, a commitment to be with whatever may arise in our experience in a friendly, inquisitive way. We need to attune our *attention* so as to remain patiently present, open, and nonreactive with whatever does show up—whether it is pleasant, unpleasant, or neutral. These two together constitute friendly attending, which you will cultivate in the next exercise.

Exercise 1.2   Friendly Attending

Begin with a brief repetition of the GAP exercise. Centering attention at your seat, sense your body's weight on the earth; say softly to yourself *grounded.* Centering attention at your head, sense the space around and above you, and tune in to subtle sounds in the environment; say softly to yourself *aware.* Centering attention in your chest, say softly to yourself *present.* Have a sense of your heart softening. As you do this, you can place your right hand gently on your heart, with the base of the thumb resting at the center of your chest.

Now imagine that you are walking alone in a forest. Suddenly you feel something looking at you from behind some trees. You realize that it is a fawn. It is mostly hidden in the undergrowth, but you can make out its moist eyes and erect ears. You know that if you make any sudden move, it will quickly disappear. Staying still just where you are, you soften your gaze and then your whole body. You are inviting the fawn to stay present. Perhaps after a while it will even come closer and show more of itself. You know you can't make it do anything, but by softening how you are in yourself, you communicate that your intentions are friendly. You are simply being gently present for the fawn, without looking for anything in particular to happen. This is the state of friendly attending.

You can also try this exercise visualizing a rabbit, a dog or cat, or a young child, whatever suits you best. The next time you encounter a shy animal or child, try this in real life.

As we practice finding the felt sense, we will undoubtedly come up against some of our inner wild animals that are not as easy to be with as a young fawn. Some of them will appear ugly or menacing—sensations and thoughts and feelings we might prefer to reject, or at least to send back into the underbrush. But these "ugly beasts" are the very creatures that have the most to teach us. They are parts of ourselves that have been in hiding: what they want more than anything is to feel recognized and accepted by us. By practicing Friendly Attending, we allow them to show up fully. This may be the only way that places where we have been stuck for a long time can become unstuck.

Here it is worth repeating Carl Rogers's dictum: It is a curious paradox that when I accept myself as I am, then I can change. We can add as a corollary: It is a curious paradox that when I accept *things* just as they are, then I can find ways to innovate and make things better.

Noticing "Something"

With the support of grounded aware presence and friendly attending, we are ready to approach the felt sense itself. It is important to note that the term *felt sense* is used today in many different contexts, and often rather loosely, lacking the precision intended by Eugene Gendlin when he introduced the term. This can be confusing: On the one hand, *felt sense* denotes something in our experience that is vague, subtle, unclear; on the other hand, it is not just any sort of vague feeling we might have. It is a particular *kind* of unclear experience that is found by bringing a particular *quality* of attention to a particular *zone* of bodily experience.

Grounded aware presence and friendly attending are the inner skills that give us access to this special zone. But once there, what exactly are we looking for? Given that felt senses are by definition unclear and quite invisible to most people, the best answer, starting out, is simply to say that we are looking for "something."

Have you ever looked at a Magic Eye picture? (They are readily available on the Internet these days.) At first you can't see anything but a jumble of computer-generated patterns and colors. But after you spend some time staring at it in a special way—which takes some experimentation to discover—a form begins to emerge, as if by magic. For a while you can't identify what the form is, but clearly there is something there. Sometimes it disappears before you can identify it, but sometimes it comes fully into focus as a three-dimensional object. At this point you have hold of it: now it is more than just something, it is a train or a kangaroo or a pretzel.

Finding the felt sense follows a similar progression: first you patiently look in the special manner of friendly attending, then you sense an unclear "something" starting to form, and finally— if and when it occurs—that something emerges into clear focus. Of course, what emerges won't be a kangaroo or a pretzel, but it will have specific qualities of shape, form, or texture, perhaps even color or temperature, that can be noticed and felt. Something concrete is present: you can sense it there in your body, and even though you may not know why it's there or what it's about, you can sense that it holds meaning.

Exercise 1.3   Noticing "Something"

Begin by simply asking yourself, "How am I?" Say whatever comes to mind: fine, OK, tired, happy, sad, excited . . .

Now ask yourself, "But how am I *really?*" This time ignore any words that arise quickly. Instead, holding in mind the question "How am I *really?*" allow there to be a gap, and simply sense inside your body with an attitude of friendly attending.

You are not answering the question from your head—that would be what you already know—but looking for a response to the question in your body. You are sensing for . . . something. You may already be noticing a particular felt sense or you may not be, but in either case there is an unclear sense of "something."

Don't rush. Go slowly and remember that all we can do is stay present and be a friendly witness to whatever comes—even when nothing comes. Especially at the beginning, felt senses tend to be quite shy; like the fawn in the woods, they are not used to being seen and need time to feel safe showing themselves. When you notice a felt sense, or something you think might be a felt sense, simply welcome it and be with it, not looking for anything more to happen right away. After a while, ask again, "How am I really?" and notice if the felt sense alters, becomes clearer, or disappears.

At any point in this process, you may experience a fresh insight, something unexpected or at a deeper level than you were in touch with before. These insights will come with a quality of freshness, a sense of *Oh!* or *Aha!* or *Now I see.* Words may come that articulate the fresh insight; at this point words can be welcomed and you can make a mental note of them, but keep it simple. Try not to go off on a long chain of thoughts about the new insight, as tempting as that might feel.

Try this exercise again, substituting different forms of the question. Instead of "How am I?" you can ask, "How am I feeling just now?" or "What does it feel like being [*say your name*] right now?" A slightly different question that can be very productive is "What's most important for me right now?" This is a bit trickier because your mind is likely to jump in with a familiar answer, but if you can stay with the nonconceptual body feel that comes in response, you are likely to receive some new information.

Whether or not new insights come at this point, the main thing is that you are starting to contact the felt sense. It is important to remember that we are all different. Some people will find the felt sense right off and recognize it as a familiar place; others will need time and repeated attempts. For a while you may be unsure whether what you are noticing inside your body really is a felt sense or just a physical sensation or some kind of imaginary phenomenon. Don't get hung up on this; just keep practicing going inside with friendly attending. Things will sort themselves out in time.

In the next two chapters you will practice three different ways of approaching the felt sense.

Chapter 2

Gateways into the Felt Sense

FELT SENSES ARE paradoxical. In a way they are always there, but since we rarely notice them, they are also *not* there. When we first bring attention into the body and sense for "something" we may notice nothing at all. Or we may sense that something is present in a bodily felt way, but it is vague, subtle, murky. In learning to find the felt sense, we have to learn to differentiate it from more common modes of experience: physical sensations, thoughts, and emotions. The good news is that each of these modes can be a gateway into the felt sense. In this chapter and the next, we will practice approaching felt senses through each of these three gates of body, mind, and emotion, beginning with the body.

The Body Gate

When we stub our toe or touch a hot stove, we experience a sudden, sharp sensation of pain. Compared to felt senses, these are purely physical sensations. They are "about" the immediate situation of toe stubbing or stove touching. Less dramatic examples would be an itch, a sore muscle, a stomachache. Of course, physical sensations can be pleasurable as well—a full belly, the touch of a friend or a lover—or they can be neutral. They are all responses to a specific stimulus or event. Usually we know exactly what is causing the sensation.

Felt senses are different. They don't seem to be responses to specific physical stimuli. Rather than having physical causes, they are connected to situations, activities, and relationships. In this way, they are more like feelings, yet different from ordinary emotions. In the next exercise, you will practice differentiating physical sensations and felt senses.

Exercise 2.1   From Physical Sensations to Felt Senses

Bring your attention to your body. Start by noticing the physical sensations wherever your body is contacting the earth—the feel of your bottom against the chair, your feet on the ground, your hand resting on the desk. Take a few moments to really notice the immediate sensory qualities you are experiencing. Notice too any places where one part of your body is touching another.

Now move your awareness all around your body and notice any kind of physical sensations: aches and pains, itches, tight spots, stiff joints. Include positive, negative, and neutral sensations. Take time to really experience each one.

Now gradually bring your awareness inside your torso—the whole area from your throat down to your bottom. First check again for any purely physical sensations anywhere in this area. Then soften your awareness and sense if there are also present some less obvious, less distinct sensations. They may not feel exactly physical, yet they are present in some way that can be felt inside the body. They will have a location, shape, texture, movement, or other tangible quality. A tight spot in the chest, a fluttery feeling in the belly, or a melting sensation around the heart are some examples, but felt senses come in endless variety and can be hard to describe in words at all.

If you don't find anything like this or aren't sure what it is you are noticing, don't worry. At this point what is important is the attitude of gently sensing inside the body—friendly attending. If you feel confused or frustrated or impatient, check if there is a body sense somewhere inside that goes along with that feeling.

The purpose of this exercise is not to make too sharp a distinction between physical sensations and felt senses. Indeed, at times they are nested together. The main point here is to learn how to shift attention from direct physical sensations to the more intangible, elusive sensations of the felt sense.

The Mind Gate

Most of us, during most of our waking hours, are involved in thinking. Whether we're expressing our thoughts in speech or silently to ourselves, there is a continuous stream of words, ideas, and images. If you're in any doubt about this, take a few minutes now to close your eyes and simply sit in silence without having any thoughts. You are unlikely to be able to sit still for more than a few seconds before some thought, memory, or daydream arises in your consciousness. This is the nature of conceptual mind—it is always going, like a radio that can't be turned off.

In working with the felt sense, we need to counteract the way in which conceptual thinking usually dominates our waking consciousness. We have to learn how to drop the story line of discursive thought in order to enter the nonconceptual felt space of direct experience. The story line is our internal narrative *about* our life experiences. It helps us make sense of our experiences and allows us to share them with others—both very important—but it is an interpretation of experience rather than the experience itself. This is a subtle point: most of the time we get along fine without differentiating direct experience from our interpretations of it. But it is a crucial difference. Like the proverbial finger pointing at the moon, our interpretation points *toward* the experience, but if we take it as the whole truth, we lose the connection to our actual, lived experience and can easily end up misleading ourselves. To contact experience directly, we need to release the story line and sense, beneath it, how our body is actually living our life situations. In the next exercise, you will practice deliberately dropping the story line.

Exercise 2.2   Dropping the Story Line

Gather your attention and bring it into your body. Take a moment to notice any unclear felt senses that may be present there, trying not to give rise to discursive thinking. After a little while, choose a topic to think deliberately about. It can be a recent event, a relationship issue, a work challenge, something in the future.

Now go ahead and think about this topic in the usual discursive way: recollecting what happened, ruminating, thinking about the future, and so forth (the word *discursive* literally means "running on about"). After about two minutes, simply let go of the whole thought process and bring your awareness into your torso. You are dropping the story line, the descriptive words and images of whatever topic you were thinking about, and bringing your attention to how things feel in your body just now.

If you find it challenging to shift gears directly from thinking to body-sensing, try first shifting your focus of attention from the story line to your breathing, noticing the physical sensations of your breath as it comes into your chest and abdomen and goes out again. Once you have moved from discursive thinking to the present-moment felt experience of breathing, you can relax the focus on your breathing and sense in the same internal space for subtle body feels. Remember, you are sensing for what is present in a nonverbal way in your experience right now. If you notice "something" try to stay with it for a while without giving rise to new thoughts.

If thoughts do arise, recognize them as thinking and let them go, gently shifting your attention back to the felt sense. After spending time with one felt sense, take time to notice if there are any others present in different spots and with different textures, shapes, or energy.

When you release the story line and find a felt sense, sometimes you will know intuitively that there is a connection between the two. Other times there may be no apparent connection. In chapter 5, we will explore in detail how to find a felt sense *about* a particular issue. For now, it makes no difference whether what you find does or doesn't seem to connect to the topic of the story line.

Dropping the story line, the ability to shift gears from discursive logic to felt sensing, is especially important. In simpler times, when you might have passed a whole day hoeing a garden plot or plowing a field, certainly the work was hard, but once you got the hang of the hoe or the plow, there was not a lot of thinking involved. There was time and space to let your thought formations disperse like clouds and to enjoy the blue sky of the moment. These days, almost everything in our lives involves *thinking*: planning ahead, multitasking, communicating with others, dealing with information overload, even daydreaming. One of the most vital skills we can develop is the ability to pause the momentum of discursive mind and experience our world—both inner and outer—directly through our senses.

Given that our lives are so thought-centric, it is no easy thing to turn off the constant talk radio of our minds. It's a bit like trying to switch from using your right hand to your left (or the other way if you are left-handed). First you have to inhibit the impulse to reach with the dominant hand; then you have to get the non-dominant hand to perform an action like brushing your teeth or writing that doesn't feel natural for it. You should expect that it will take repeated practice to become proficient at dropping the story line, and there are likely to be times when it is uncomfortable. Be gentle with yourself; adding to the discomfort by getting frustrated or discouraged is counterproductive.

Mindfulness meditation, which is really a kind of basic training in detaching from discursive thought, can be a great support for finding the felt sense. Dropping our story lines, creating a gap in discursive mind, pausing the momentum of thinking—whatever we choose to call it—is a process of self-cultivation. It is a gentle discipline of becoming familiar with the open, nonconceptual space in ourselves that is always available once we know how to find and rest in it. My Buddhist teacher, Chögyam Trungpa Rinpoche, used to talk about "going back to square zero." Square zero is this inner space that is empty of specific content yet full of fresh possibility. It is a "full emptiness" that provides a home base, a place we can come back to when we find ourselves off-kilter, rest for a while, and then make a fresh start.

Chapter 3

The Feeling beneath
the Feeling

Oꜰ ᴛʜᴇ ᴛʜʀᴇᴇ ɢᴀᴛᴇꜱ, the third—emotion—is the most challenging. This is because ordinary feelings and emotions are the hardest to differentiate from felt senses. As its name suggests, a felt sense involves some kind of feeling, but it is not the usual kind of feeling we associate with emotion words like *angry, sad,* or *happy.* Understanding this difference is a key to success in finding and learning from the felt sense.

Ordinary emotions are a blend of physical, mental, and affective (felt) experiences. When you get angry, there are physical changes, such as muscles tensing and feeling hot; there is a conceptual story line about why you're angry; and there is a felt-sense component, which you're probably not conscious of. As we will see, a felt sense, once it is recognized, can "feel" very different from the emotion you started with. It exists at another, more subtle level. A felt sense is the feeling that lies beneath the feeling.

For example, as I sit at my desk, writing, my dog Luna suddenly starts barking loudly toward the front door. A man is delivering a package on the porch. I feel a rush of anger at the dog, and I turn and bark back at her, "Luna, be quiet! Come here! Lie down!" But if I step back from my anger and check what's going on in my body, I notice an achy, squeezing sensation at the center of my chest. This is a felt sense. Giving that achy place some friendly, curious attention, I discern a sense of vulnerability there, and a need for self-protection. I have been intensely focused on my writing, and the barking threatens to interrupt my train of thought.

What I've realized so far may seem obvious—I've been interrupted while working and I'm upset about it. But there's more here. I now have enough self-awareness to question whether shouting at the dog is the skillful response: Does it prevent me from being interrupted, or does it in fact contribute to the interruption? Is this the way I *want* to behave toward my dog? Is my gentle, loving, and loyal Luna *trying* to interrupt me or just doing her canine duty? Now I have the space to see more appropriate ways to respond: I can choose to stay focused on my writing, knowing the barking will soon subside, as it always does; I can gently but firmly reassure the dog that everything is all right; I can go with the dog to the door and open it, letting her see that nothing is amiss, and perhaps pick up my package at the same time.

But there is still more here: I can now question why my reaction to this small disruption was so strong in the first place. Directing friendly attention to the felt sense, this achy, squeezed sensation in my chest, I receive the spontaneous insight that at some preconscious level I fear that if I lose my train of thought, I'll never get it back. I will be "lost." Now I remember the panicky feeling of being lost in the woods, something that happened to me twice when I was a young child. With this insight, I am able to soothe that young child part of myself—of course getting lost and not knowing how to get back to the family is scary when you are six years old!

I am able to see now that the surge of emotion triggered by my dog's barking was more from that old fear of getting lost than from the present situation. Yes, getting interrupted is irritating, but have I actually lost my train of thought irretrievably? Of course not: my present-day, grown-up self knows perfectly well how to refocus on my work and pick up where I left off. It even knows that after an unexpected interruption like this, I'm likely to get fresh insights and be able to say something worthwhile I wouldn't have had access to if Luna hadn't jolted me out of my rut!

This seemingly insignificant episode highlights the difference between an emotion (sudden anger) and what the felt sense beneath it can reveal (fear of being lost). It also nicely illustrates the series of small steps that are involved in first finding a felt sense and then eliciting new, helpful information from it. In chapter 5, you will go through all of these steps using an episode from your own life. In the following exercise, you will practice just the crucial step of searching "underneath" an emotion in order to find a felt sense.

Exercise 3.1   The Feeling beneath the Feeling

Start with the three GAP steps. Then, as in the previous exercise, begin by bringing to mind a situation in your life. This time, choose something that you know has an emotional charge to it—something that makes you angry is a good place to begin.

However, a note of caution here: You want to bring to mind something that evokes anger but not so much that you become overwhelmed by it. If the emotion is too strong, you won't be able to get enough distance to search underneath it for the felt sense. So, if you are prone to being flooded by strong emotions, instead of a situation that provokes anger, try starting with something that is merely irritating, annoying, or frustrating.

Relive the situation in your mind. At the same time, be attentive to any physical changes—constriction, agitation, heat, rising or sinking sensations—that signal the presence of emotion. Depending on whether or not you are someone who easily becomes emotional, you may have to experiment to get enough felt emotion so that you can experience it in your body but not so much that it overwhelms you. Once the emotion is clearly present, take time to notice specifically where and how it is affecting your body.

Next, invite into your awareness a subtler body sense of the situation. To do this, you have to both drop the story line and step outside of the raw energy of the emotion it has evoked. This is a question of getting the right distance: enough that you aren't trapped inside the emotion but not so distant that it's not there at all. See if you can find a region of experience that lies below the emotion. What is important here is your willingness to sense deeper in yourself by means of gentle, nonreactive friendly attending. After a while, a felt sense may emerge. It will have its own bodily felt qualities such as tightness or heat or "like a small ball in my belly," but this body feel will be more subtle than a tight jaw, a pounding heart, or constricted breathing. The felt sense may also have an emotional tone like fear or sadness or vulner-ability that is quite different from the emotion you started out with.*

Getting to the felt senses lying beneath the raw emotions trig-gered by events in our lives involves a process of disidentification. When we are in the midst of an emotion, we are identified with it. Instead of us having the emotion, the emotion *has us*. There may be times when being completely absorbed in an emotion is exactly where we want to be, but it is also well known that strong

---

* The "feeling beneath the feeling" isn't always different from the original emotion; sometimes this process is more about staying with the bodily felt quality of the original emotion—fear, for example—and allowing more facets and subtleties of it to emerge.

emotions affect our perception of reality and our judgment. We say and do things that we later wish we could undo or do differently. Knowing how to disidentify, to get some space between us and the emotion, is a skill vital to our long-term welfare.

You can picture the process of disidentification as if you are stepping back from the emotion, placing the emotion somewhere outside of you, rising above the emotion, making yourself larger than the emotion, or putting a box around the emotion. These are all metaphors for the change of perspective involved in disidentifying. Consider which of these metaphors best fits you—or consult your felt sense and come up with your own.

It is helpful to practice the three gateway exercises in chapters 2 and 3 several times. You can do them all in a single session or one at a time. It's fine to spend more time on the ones that seem to work best for you. You can take a break from any exercise that is confusing, frustrating, or just unproductive, but try to come back to it after some days or weeks. Something may have shifted in you in the meantime that will give you better results.

Chapter 4

Cultivating Felt Senses

I WANT TO BEGIN this chapter by pausing to ask, "How's it going?" Imagine that I am right there with you now, checking in about your experience of working with the instructions in this book so far. How would you answer me? Write down what you would say in a sentence or two.

Now take the same question, about how all of this is going for you, and dive deeper with it.

Exercise 4.1   "How's It Going?"

Take as much time as you need to come into your felt-sense zone.

When ready, ask yourself inside, "How is the whole experience of reading this book and practicing finding the felt sense going for me so far?" Pause and allow a felt sense to form in response to the question. Whatever comes, welcome it and sense how it really feels in your body. Let it simply be present.

Now take more time to go over in your mind what you remember about your experience with this book up to this point. You might begin with whatever circumstance prompted you to start reading it in the first place, remembering what you imagined it would be about or what you were hoping to get from it. Then recall your first impressions as you started reading. What experiences have you had doing the exercises? What insights have come? What obstacles? What needs in you are getting met, and which are not? What's your sense of where all this may be leading? What else comes to you about the whole experience?

Now, having sensed how your body is holding your experience of this book up to this point, ask yourself inside, "How am I feeling about going further?" Acknowledge any feelings of hesitation, discomfort, or confusion, and also sense your appetite and energy for moving forward.

Finally, imagine again that I am right there asking you, "How is all this, your experience of working with this book, so far?" What would you now say to me? Write down your answer and compare it to the first one. Did any fresh or deeper understanding come?

Mindful Focusing is not only for solving problems. It is also a wonderful way to contemplate our experiences in life, appreciate them more deeply, and gain new insights. And now, having contemplated in this way, are you ready to travel further? Remember, at any point you can go back to earlier exercises; learning is an iterative process, and it isn't necessary or even possible to understand everything perfectly before moving on.

In chapters 2 and 3, we learned how to differentiate felt senses from physical sensations, thoughts, and emotions; we also used each of those as a gateway or stepping-stone to finding the felt sense. If the difference between felt-sensing and those other modes of experiencing is not yet entirely clear, it should become clearer as you do the next few exercises.

At the beginning of a practice session, there are three basic ways to evoke a felt sense to spend time with. You can start by noticing what felt senses your body is already holding. Or, you can ask yourself inside, "What wants my attention just now?" Or, you can start with a specific issue or situation that you know you want to explore using the felt sense. In this chapter and the next, you will become familiar with each of these approaches.

Exercise 4.2 Noticing What Your Body Is Already Holding

Take time to really come into your body. Go through the GAP steps to settle into a state of grounded aware presence. Then shift your attention to your breath. Notice the feeling of air entering and leaving your lungs. Feel the sensations of your chest and abdomen expanding and contracting, from your throat all the way down to your lower belly. Then shift attention from the sensations of breathing to the entire inner space where breathing happens. Rest your awareness there gently with an attitude of friendly attending. Notice anything inside that space that is present in a felt-sense way.

If nothing seems to be there at first, give it some time. When you notice any kind of unclear inner sensation, stay with it for a while. Keep it company. Explore and appreciate its felt qualities, noticing its shape, texture, movement, color, or temperature. Welcome its presence and get to know it. If you find yourself going off into thoughts or fantasies, gently bring your attention back to whatever is present in your body in an unclear but somatically felt way.

When you bring your attention inside and try to notice a felt sense, you may first find a particular issue, problem, need, or want that your body is holding. This is fine, because any issue can be a stepping-stone to a felt sense. However, you need to resist the temptation to think about the situation in the usual way. Instead, just name the general topic as simply as possible—"my project at work"; "what happened between Mary and me"; "where to spend Thanksgiving." A good trick here is to add the words *all that about* to the topic you name. This helps to counter any impulse to go into the details. "All that about Mary and me" covers the whole situation. As you summarize the issue in this way, notice what felt sense comes in your body. Even if it is very vague or slight, just be with that felt sense. If the particulars of the situation start coming to mind, gently let go of them and return with friendly attending to the felt sense.

For example, I have to give a presentation in a few hours, and I'm feeling a bit nervous about it. I say to myself, "All that about my presentation," naming the topic without actually thinking about it. Sensing beneath that, after a few seconds have passed, I notice a subtle constriction across my chest and into my shoulders. I invite this to become more present. I sit with it, keeping it company, with an attitude of friendly attending. From here many things might develop—the constriction might become stronger, or it might change or go away, or I might notice another, deeper felt sense lying below it.

A second way to get started with felt-sensing is simply to ask yourself inside, "What wants my attention just now?" Before posing this question, it is important that you are already attending inwardly, aware of your visceral space, so that the answer won't be coming only from your head. You may get a response that is an issue, an emotion, or a felt sense. It doesn't matter as long as it comes from the body.

Exercise 4.3 "What Wants My Attention Just Now?"

Take whatever time you need to bring awareness inside your body. Then ask gently, "What wants my attention just now?" If an answer comes right away, check whether your body sense confirms that this is really what needs attention at this moment or if there is something deeper or less obvious there. If no answer comes right away, just wait and see if something bubbles up after a while. If you get more than one answer to the question—you may be holding several concerns at the moment—let your body decide which one would feel right to spend time with. If what comes is a problem needing a solution, instead of trying to jump to the solution right away, see if you can get a felt sense of the situation as a whole. How does it feel in your body?

In the following chapters we will explore how to enter into dialogue with a felt sense to gain fresh insights, solve problems, make decisions, and find action steps, but before doing that, it is essential to have the ability to simply stay with a felt sense in a friendly, inquisitive way without needing anything more to happen (without what Keats called "irritable reaching after fact and reason"). This is the getting-to-know-you phase, welcoming the felt sense to simply be present before trying to do anything with it.

The next chapter looks at the third way to invite felt senses, beginning from specific problems or challenges we already have in mind.

Chapter 5

Working with Situations

Both of the techniques for engaging your felt sense presented in the previous chapter—bringing awareness inside your torso area to sense what your body is already holding, and starting by asking inside, "What wants my attention just now?"—can lead to important, even life-changing insights. That said, finding the felt sense is a powerful and radically different way to approach the specific challenges we are facing in our lives. Often it is the situation itself—a problem, emotion, action block, decision, work project, relationship issue, creative undertaking—that will prompt us to engage our felt sense. Once you are familiar with the process, felt-sensing can happen in a minute or less. This means it can often be applied in real time, right as situations are happening. But to learn and gain confidence in engaging your felt sense, you will want to devote some longer, uninterrupted sessions to practice.

The key to working with a situation through your felt sense is dropping or releasing its story line and attending to the feeling in your body. However, in dropping the story line, we don't want to totally abandon the situation we are trying to work with. Even as we let go of its details, our emotions, and our ideas about it, we still want to hold on to its essential texture and energy. The situation has to remain present for us in a bodily felt way, even as the specifics recede from awareness.

There is a kind of paradox here: letting go and holding on at the same time. It is like the gap in a meaningful conversation when two people stop talking and feel the issue and each other's presence more intensely. Eugene Gendlin calls this paradoxical process "holding and letting." Here is how he describes it in his major philosophical work, *A Process Model,* using the technical term "direct referent" in place of felt sense:

> In direct referent formation one both keeps the situation the same, and one also lets it change. One keeps it the same *by holding* the relevance, the point, the sense of the whole thing, the same. It is *this* situation (and all that is involved in it), which I wish to sense as a whole. I hold on to this relevance. But also, I await the coming of a new kind of feel, the felt sense of the whole business. I can only *let* it come, I can't make it. In letting it come, I allow my body-feel to stir, to move, to do whatever it does independently of my deliberate control, while I do employ my deliberate control to keep the situation, the relevance.[1]

"Holding and letting" lies at the heart of Gendlin's technique of Focusing, or finding the felt sense. It is the core dynamic of friendly attending. Indeed, it is the defining feature of all true contemplative practices.

I will have more to say about the philosophical and contemplative theory underlying Mindful Focusing in later chapters. For now, let's stay with the main aim of this book, which is cultivating your own direct experience.

Exercise 5.1   Starting with a Situation

Decide on a situation to work with—anything that is alive for you right now. Then let go of it completely while you take as much time as you need to come into grounded aware presence. Then invite the chosen situation back into your awareness. Let different particulars of the situation come to mind, recollecting enough of the story line to make it vividly present, while at the same time staying gently aware of what's happening in your body. When the situation, problem, or challenge is clearly present in awareness, release the story line and notice what felt sense it has brought in your body. If there is no felt sense after a while, or if the felt sense disappears, you can go back to the story line and repeat the process.

Sometimes the felt sense will lead you away from the chosen topic, perhaps to an entirely different situation. When this happens, follow the felt sense! Remember, felt-sensing is always about what is alive—in process—in your life right now. One reason we become stuck when trying to accomplish a conscious purpose is that there is something else, perhaps at a deeper level or "off to the side," that needs our attention before any forward movement can occur.

It is also not uncommon when trying to get in touch with the felt sense of a challenging situation to first encounter a felt sense of the way in which we are *protecting that part from being seen.* Just as the body protects a wound by tightening up around it and making the surrounding area painful to touch, our felt sense may tighten or raise the alarm when a vulnerable area begins to be touched. In this case, it is important first to bring your friendly attending to the part that's doing the protecting. This part may manifest as a sense of tightness, thickness, heat, or sensitivity. Recognizing and bringing friendly attention to it helps it relax. When the protecting part relaxes, the felt sense of the challenging situation itself can then emerge.

Sometimes the protecting part is not ready to give up its role so easily. It is important not to fight with it. Instead, try giving it empathy. You can say to it, "Of course you want to protect this place that feels so vulnerable [bad, scary, shameful]!" All felt senses deserve our respect, even those we would prefer to be rid of. Each of them is there for its own good reason. Perhaps the reason is outdated or not in touch with the big picture, but this part of us will keep striving to do its job until it has been recognized. It is by being recognized, heard, and treated kindly that these deeply embedded protective parts are able to get unstuck and become active contributors to positive change.

Perhaps you have heard the parable of the contest between the wind and the sun to show which one of them could separate a man from his coat. The wind goes first, but the harder it blows, the more tightly the man wraps himself in his coat. Then the sun goes, merely shining and warming the air until the man happily sheds his coat. Friendly attending is like the sun.

Chapter 6

Bringing the Felt Sense
into Focus

FELT SENSES START OUT vague, fuzzy, murky, subtle, unclear. This is like the experience of looking through a pair of binoculars that is out of focus. You see vague shapes and colors but can't recognize what you're looking at. What do you do? You continue looking through the eyepieces and at the same time rotate the focus wheel until things become clear. In working with felt senses, we follow a similar process, adjusting our awareness until the felt sense comes into focus.*

However, there is a difference. When the view through the binoculars comes into focus, we recognize familiar objects that we can name: a tree, a house, an osprey. When a felt sense comes into focus, it is a special kind of object that by its very nature can't be named with a noun like *tree* or *bird*. The felt sense always *is and has more* than can be categorized. This is another way of saying that the felt sense is fundamentally nonconceptual. It also

---

*This is why Eugene Gendlin gave the felt-sensing process the name Focusing. Because the word *focusing* suggests the conventional idea of concentrating one's attention—"Focus!"—which is virtually the opposite of friendly attending, I prefer *finding the felt sense* or just *felt-sensing.*

explains why felt senses are different from the common emotions that do have names like anger, fear, happiness, and sadness. Nonetheless, felt senses *can* be described with words, if instead of using nouns we use adjectives.

Each felt sense has its own unique, specific qualities. Imagine meeting a new person: At first you don't know the person's name, you don't know "who they are," but you are perfectly able to observe and describe their qualities. They are tall, short, or of average height; their hair is dark or light, long or short, curly or straight; they are slender or heavyset; they are young or old, happy or sad, outgoing or shy, and so on.

Now imagine that you are describing this new person to a friend. As you name each of the person's qualities, your friend builds up a clearer picture of what this person is like. The still-nameless person begins to come into focus for your friend. Perhaps at a certain point your friend realizes you are describing somebody whom they know. Now all at once your friend can tell you the person's name and a great deal more about them that you weren't able to discover just by observation.

Similarly, when a felt sense is present in an unclear way, we can help it come into focus by naming its qualities. Because it is something that is bodily felt, the words we use to describe it will evoke tangible, physical sensations: *tight, hard, fluttery, warm, round, dark, hollow, sinking, flowing,* and so on. Sometimes an image or metaphor will capture the feeling inside: *a hard ball, like a shield, like flames.* Sometimes it will take a combination of quality words and images to describe the felt sense: *prickly like a cactus, like a dark heavy stone, expanding like a balloon.* At other times a hand gesture, movement, or change in body posture works best.

In the following exercise you can experiment with using descriptive adjectives, images, and gestures to bring your felt sense into clearer focus.

NO POSTAGE
NECESSARY
IF MAILED
IN THE
UNITED STATES

BUSINESS REPLY MAIL
FIRST-CLASS MAIL   PERMIT NO. 11494   BOSTON MA

POSTAGE WILL BE PAID BY ADDRESSEE

SHAMBHALA PUBLICATIONS
PO BOX 170358
BOSTON MA 02117-9812

SHAMBHALA PUBLICATIONS

If you'd like to receive a copy of our latest catalogue of books and audios, please fill out and return this card. It's easy—the postage is already paid!

Or, if you'd prefer, you can e-mail us at CustomerCare@shambhala.com, sign up online at www.shambhala.com/newsletter, or call toll-free (888) 424-2329.

NAME _____

ADDRESS _____

CITY / STATE / ZIP / COUNTRY _____

E-MAIL _____

And by also giving us your e-mail address, you'll automatically be signed up to receive news about new releases, author events, and special offers!

Exercise 6.1 Describing the Felt Sense

Go through the preparatory steps of bringing awareness to the body and becoming present in yourself, taking as much time as feels right. When you feel ready, find or invite a felt sense that you want to spend time with. You can do this by bringing awareness directly to your felt-sense zone, by starting with a known situation, or by asking gently inside, "What wants my attention just now?" If you start with a situation, such as a relationship problem or work challenge, recollect enough of its specifics—the story line—to make it present in your experience right now. Then drop the story line, bring awareness inside, and attend to whatever felt sense your body is holding.

Be present with the felt sense and welcome it to be present with you. Be gentle, don't rush, don't react judgmentally, and don't get preoccupied with a train of thought. Just be there—friendly attending—with whatever unclear "something" you can sense right now. After a while, try out a word, phrase, image, or gesture to capture how the felt sense appears or feels. It is essential to keep the felt sense present as you check to see whether the word, image, or gesture really fits. If it isn't quite right, keep adjusting the description until the felt sense lets you know, "Yes, that says it, that's just how it feels!"

Have you had the experience of choosing a picture frame? Your eye may be attracted to a certain shape, color, or texture, but in order to know if it's right, you have to hold a sample of the frame up to the picture itself. Often you have to try several different frames before settling on the one that best fits the picture because it complements the visual image and makes it "pop." The felt sense is like the picture, and the description of the felt sense is like the frame. Holding them together in your awareness, check whether the word, image, phrase, or gesture you've come up with is the best possible fit for this particular felt sense. As with the picture, a good fit will make the felt sense stand out more clearly. Remember, you can always change the frame if it doesn't fit right—but don't change the felt sense to fit the frame!

The process of comparing descriptive words, images, or gestures to the felt sense is called resonating. It is like tuning an instrument. If your first attempt at description doesn't attune perfectly with the felt sense, keep adjusting it until it does. You will know you have a good fit when the felt sense itself feels properly recognized.

For this exercise and others in this book, you may find it helpful to have a journal in which you can record key words, images, and insights, either as they arise or at the end of your session.

Chapter 7

Requesting Insight from the Felt Sense

HAVING BROUGHT the felt sense into focus by describing and resonating, you have established a respectful, caring relationship with a part of yourself that embodies an undifferentiated, holistic knowing about your past experience, present situation, and future direction. It contains *more* than what your conceptual mind already knows. Sometimes this wordless body feel is all you need in order to go forward, but often you will want to take the next step and bring forth a conceptual understanding that articulates new insights and options for action. Now that the felt sense is fully present, you are in a position to invite it to translate its body-knowing into mind-knowing. We do this through empathic inquiry, a gentle process of addressing open-ended questions to the felt sense itself.

A word about the word *insight*: As used here it means "freshly realized meaning." Insight includes both the preverbal body feel of some newly emergent meaning and the articulation of that new meaning in words and ideas. In Focusing, insights can arise first as a new body feel or first as a new idea or as both simultaneously. Often they come with an "Aha!" of recognition and a palpable easing, release, or shift in the felt sense. Sometimes these "felt shifts" are accompanied by a sigh or deepened breathing, by changes in posture, or by tears. All of these are indicators that there has been real movement in how the body is holding a situation.

The next exercise, Empathic Inquiry, builds on Exercise 1.3: Noticing "Something." The objective there was to penetrate to a felt sense by challenging our reflexive answer to the question "How are you?" We did this by reframing the question as "But how am I *really*?" Here you will repeat the same steps and then go deeper by asking additional questions directly to the felt sense.

Exercise 7.1   Empathic Inquiry

Begin by simply asking yourself, "How am I?" Say whatever comes to mind: fine, OK, tired, happy, sad, excited . . .

Now ask yourself, "But how am I *really*?" This time ignore any words that come quickly. Instead, holding in mind the question "How am I really?" allow there to be a gap, and simply sense inside your body with an attitude of friendly attending.

If no felt sense comes, or if another verbal answer comes, repeat the question while attending to your inner body space. Keep asking, "But how am I really?" until you notice a bodily response—something that stirs or forms freshly when you pose the question, or perhaps something that has been there all along unnoticed.

Welcome and be with whatever body sense is there. After a while, see if you can come up with a simple description— adjective(s), image, metaphor, or gesture—that captures the felt sense. Check if the description resonates with the felt sense itself. If the fit doesn't feel quite right, adjust the description until it does.

You can include an emotion word in your description if the felt sense resonates with it, but be specific. For example, if the felt sense brings the word *sad*, ask inside, "What kind of sad?" See if there is a modifier, an adjective or an image that tells what kind of sadness is there just now. You'll know you're on the right track if what comes is an unexpected or unusual combination of words like "jittery-sad," "achy-sad," "sad like an overstretched rubber band."

When the description fits the felt sense clearly, move on to the empathic inquiry stage by posing a friendly question to the felt sense. You might simply ask, "What in my life is like this?" Or, more specifically, "Is there anything going on in my life that brings this kind of [jittery-sad, achy-sad, overstretched rubber band, etc.] feeling?" If you already know that the felt sense relates to a particular situation, you can frame the question as "What about this situation makes it so [achy-sad, etc.]?"

Use emotion words only if they really touch the quality of the felt sense. Otherwise, just ask directly, "What in my life feels like an overstretched rubber band?" or "What is it about this situation that makes me feel so overstretched?" Remember that often there is a period of silence before an answer bubbles up from the felt sense.

A good question to pose when you're working with a complex, uncomfortable situation is "What is the worst part of all this?" Allow a gap after the question and see what response comes from the felt sense. Like a young child, the felt sense may not respond to the question at all. When this happens, try not to be frustrated or offended; just drop the question and go back to friendly attending. Then try a different question or a different way of asking the same question. For example, if there is no response to "What is the worst of all this?" try addressing the felt sense directly, as if it were a child: "Is there something you are fearful about?" Or "What is it that you are wanting?" Leave a gap and see if the felt sense itself responds with words, or if a fresh insight comes that you can put into words.

With this exercise, we have arrived at the heart of Mindful Focusing, actually entering into dialogue with the felt sense and, if it cooperates, getting new information from it. Because this involves first recognizing the felt sense, then using describing and resonating to bring it into focus, and then eliciting fresh insight through empathic inquiry, it is likely to take some time.

It is also a good practice to ask yourself, "But how am I *really?*" anytime someone asks you how you are. After giving the usual sort of reply—"I'm well, thank you," "Doing OK," "Good"—ask yourself inwardly how you *really* feel and see what shows up. You may even be comfortable sharing some of what comes with the other person, which is a powerful way to build trust and deepen relationships. In part 2, I'll say more about how the felt sense functions in relationships; the point here is that you can use these everyday exchanges as a reminder to check in with your felt sense.

Finally, it bears repeating that sometimes the best thing to do with a felt sense is not to pose questions to it or even describe its qualities but simply to keep it company empathically for as long as feels right to you—or to it.

Chapter *8*

Small Steps, Felt Shifts, and Appreciating What Came

FORWARD MOVEMENT in the body's process typically involves a series of small shifts rather than one sudden illumination. It is crucial that we be sensitive to these slight shifts in the felt sense and take ample time to fully appreciate them and absorb whatever insight has come before trying to go further.

To illustrate this process before having you try it for yourself, I invite you to accompany me as I contemplate a situation in my own life. As you read the following account, there are several things I would like you to notice. One is how small the individual steps can be, so slight that ordinarily we wouldn't notice any movement at all and would just feel stuck. (I'm not saying that larger body-shifts and breakthrough insights never happen; they can and will, but they are prepared for by a series of small shifts, often in apparently unrelated aspects of our lives, until a tipping point is reached.) Second, I want you to appreciate the amount of patience, gentleness, and self-empathy that this kind of inner work calls for. And third, recognize the importance of *receiving* what comes—really feeling it, taking it in, letting it permeate your body-mind. This is akin to properly digesting your food after chewing, tasting, and swallowing it, so that it enters your system and nurtures you in ways you are not even conscious of.

Recently I did a session of felt-sensing on a writing project I'm working on with a young man with whom I am close. He has been very slow about completing his part of the project, and I've been feeling frustrated and impatient to have it done. Below I re-create the steps in my process and comment on some key aspects.

> I become aware of tension in my throat and shoulders [noticing "something"]. I take time to acknowledge this physical sensation, and then I sense for a subtler quality of body-knowing [felt sense] lying within or below it. The word "blocked" comes to mind [describing]. When I check this against the felt sense [resonating], it changes to "held up." This seems to fit the felt sense just right.
>
> I keep this felt sense of "held up" patient company for a while [more friendly attending]. Then, I gently pose the question, "What is it about this situation with my young friend that feels so held up?" [empathic inquiry]. Without reverting to what I already know—his slowness and my impatience— I let the question hover in the air and wait to see what may arise from the felt sense itself. What comes after a bit is the insight "I've put a lot of time into this project myself, I'm pleased with my work, and it's important to me now to be able to share it with others." I check this statement with the felt sense (more resonating). Yes, that fits, and now I notice an easing in the tension around my throat and shoulders [small step, felt shift].

This first bit of movement came from simply reframing the problem. Instead of just feeling frustration, I got some information about the reasons behind the frustration. Recognizing these reasons as appropriate to the situation increased my self-awareness and, in turn, allowed me to feel self-empathy. While self-empathy on its own is not yet a solution, it subtly shifts the way I'm holding the problem. It acknowledges the validity of my own experience and, importantly, doesn't blame the other person.

> I return to the felt sense, noticing that although the tension around my throat and shoulders hasn't disappeared, there is now more space and softness around it. I ask inside, "Is there something more involved here?" [empathic inquiry]. Again I wait, just holding the question.

Holding the question means staying with the feel of the question while not actually answering it, as you might stay with the tone of a gong for a long time after it has been struck. If the feel of the question starts to fade, you can refresh it by saying the question to yourself again. If there is no response from the felt sense, you can also try rewording the question. For example, if nothing came in response to "Is there something more involved here?" I might address the felt sense more directly, asking it gently, "What's still making you tense in there?"

> After a while, a fresh realization comes, from a deeper level of the felt sense: what is really at stake here is less about the project than about my relationship with this young man [insight]. I am in touch now with how deeply I care about him, with my knowing about his ongoing difficulties in getting things done, and with my concern about how all this may affect his feelings of self-worth and his success in life. With this change in perspective [small step] comes a larger shift in my felt sense: the tension in my throat and shoulders releases [felt shift], and at the same time I notice a knotted feeling in the area of my solar plexus.

When one felt sense releases, often another will appear, signaling that there are other dimensions to the situation that we were not consciously aware of.

I take time to sense gently into the knotted feeling [friendly attending]. After a while, the words "achy-sad" come [describing]. I check these words against the felt sense and confirm that they fit [resonating]. I recognize this as a familiar feeling of vulnerability [small step], but it isn't clear yet how it relates to this situation. What first comes to mind is "I need to confront my friend and ask him what's getting in the way of his completing his part of the project." But when I check this against the achy-sad place, it doesn't fit [resonating]. It doesn't meet the need implied in my own feeling of vulnerability.

After attending to the achy-sad place a bit longer, a key insight comes: I myself have had difficulties getting things done, especially when I was a younger person. As I realize this [not so small step], my impulse to confront my friend softens into a feeling of compassion, and I'm aware of a sense of relief, and release, in the knotted, achy-sad place [felt shift]. I pause here and take this in, feeling more deeply both the insight and the changed felt sense [appreciating what came].

It is important not to rush ahead, even with the good energy that has come.

After a while, I turn to the felt sense again and ask, "Is there more?" I notice that the knot, although softer, hasn't completely dissolved and is also tinged with fear. I ask it, "What are you fearing?" Another small insight and body-shift comes: I fear that if the project remains incomplete, things will end up worse than before: my friend may internalize the experience as a failure on his part as well as a disappointment to me, and it may become a shadow on our future relationship.

Now I'm sitting with a conundrum: it feels more important than ever to make progress with the project, and at the same time I don't want to push things forward in a way that would undermine his self-esteem, for example by taking over the project and completing it on my own.

At the heart of most thorny problems are two or more sides or interests that appear to be in direct contradiction.

> I reflect on what I know so far: our relationship is more important than the end product; therefore, the main thing is to keep communicating about the project, patiently and as skillfully as I can [small step]. This feels right, bringing a further release in the felt sense, and yet a small knot of achy-sadness still remains. The conflicting sides—getting it done versus not undermining my friend—are still in tension. There is something more here, about how to hold this paradox. Ah! Now it comes. Even though I am clear that our relationship is the primary thing, and that I am committed to continuing to communicate with as much patience and skill as I can muster, and that I want very much for this experience to be a success for both of us, at the end of the day I cannot control the outcome [insight]. It is not in my power to rescue or change my friend, who is, after all, an adult.
>
> With this, the knotted feeling in my solar plexus dissolves. I am left with a softened feeling of sadness tinged with fear, but now I know exactly what it is about, and this feeling itself will now inform and support, rather than inhibit, my intention to be patient and skillful in meeting the intricate challenges of the situation. I take time to fully receive all that has come, letting it permeate my body and mind [appreciating what came].
>
> I finish by returning to the simplicity of grounded aware presence, then raising my gaze and extending awareness out into space. Freshly experiencing details of the environment, I sense my presence in and as part of the larger world.

I have described my inner steps in considerable detail to illustrate how the felt-sensing process often unfolds in a series of small perceptions and felt shifts. In this example, I may not have solved the problem I began with—how to bring the project to completion—and it might still fail. But I have been changed. Not only my understanding of the situation is different, but the very way in which my body experiences it has changed. I can feel the difference, and how I now behave in the situation will change accordingly. I can move ahead with the project *including* my uncertainty about its outcome.

In the second half of the book, we will look more closely at how finding your felt sense leads to positive changes in behavior. Right now I invite you to explore the themes of small steps, felt shifts, and appreciating what came by contemplating something in your own life. Since you have now been introduced to all the basic steps of Mindful Focusing, you can use as a guideline the Mindful Focusing protocol that follows. As indicated in the final step, "transitioning back to the world," complete this and future sessions by taking time to return to simple grounded aware presence and gently reconnect with the world around you, appreciating it freshly, before going on to whatever activity may be next for you.

Mindful Focusing Protocol

Here is an outline of the basic steps of Mindful Focusing. You can refer to it as you practice. However, it is only a guideline. Focusing is an organic, freshly occurring process; you can skip steps or parts of steps, or let them come in a different order. Your practice will evolve over time. Do what feels right for you!

1. Grounded Aware Presence (GAP)
   - center attention at your base (grounded), head (aware), and heart (presence)
   - (brief version) settle your body, drop thinking, bring awareness inside your torso
2. Finding the felt sense
   - assume an attitude of friendly attending

- notice what your body is holding—"something" or
  "something in me" (or)
- ask, "What wants my attention just now?" (or)
- start with a situation
  - recollect the situation freshly for a minute or two
  - drop the story line
  - sense for the feeling beneath the feeling
3. Bringing the felt sense into focus
   - describe its felt qualities using a word, phrase, meta-
     phor, image, or gesture
   - resonate—does the description fit? does the felt sense
     like it?
4. Empathic inquiry
   - pose a question and wait for the felt sense to respond
     - "What makes it [you, me] feel so _____?"
     - "What is the worst part of all this?"
     - "What is it [are you, am I] fearing?"
     - "What is it [are you, am I] wanting?"
5. Appreciating what came
   - notice and receive any small steps, felt shifts, and
     insights
   - after receiving, ask inside, "Is there more?"
   - choose when to stop for now
     - journal (recommended)
   - thank your body
6. Transitioning back to the world
   - return to a sense of grounded aware presence
   - gently open your awareness outward; notice and
     freshly appreciate your surroundings
   - sense your own presence within and as part of the
     larger environment

Chapter 9

Cultivating Self-Empathy and Defusing the Inner Critic

As outlined in the Mindful Focusing protocol, we have now covered all the fundamental steps of Mindful Focusing. I want to emphasize that these steps do not constitute a fixed formula for how the practice should always be done. They have been presented as a road map into new territory, a basic skill set for a different way of working with the manifold challenges all of us face. In part 2, "Living Life Forward," we will look at how to apply these skills in specific contexts of daily life such as relationships, work, learning, and creative process. As you gain mastery of the basics and apply them to the material of your own life, you will find what works best for you and develop refinements and new steps not covered here.

To complete the presentation of the basic method of Mindful Focusing, there are two additional important topics that are not so much specific steps in the technique as they are recurring themes: self-empathy and the inner critic.

Self-empathy is a particular application of empathy, the intention or attitude that underlies both friendly attending and empathic inquiry. In friendly attending, we bring a gentle, caring attitude to whatever arises in our felt sense, especially the difficult places that come with uncomfortable feelings like fear, anger, shame, guilt, and so on. Self-empathy means bringing that same attitude to oneself as the person who is undergoing these difficult feelings. This is like the difference between feeling empathy for someone who is sick and feeling empathy for ourselves when we take on the burden of caring for a sick person. It is having the wisdom to acknowledge the impact that caring for a sick friend or family member is having on *us* and figuring out how to take care of ourselves *as part of* helping the other person.

Exercise 9.1 Self-Empathy

Think of something about yourself that you wish were different, such as having too much work, not having enough income, loneliness, interpersonal conflict, procrastination, a disturbing memory, addictive behavior, a health concern, fits of anger, or periods of depression.

Begin by thinking about the issue in the usual way and notice how that makes you feel. Then imagine for a moment that you are standing outside your own body, looking at yourself as if at another person holding those same thoughts and feelings. Feel empathy for that person and their difficulties.

Now bring the person close and embrace them, offering them care and comfort. The compassionate you is embracing the suffering you. This is self-empathy.

Self-empathy is not feeling sorry for oneself. It is feeling compassion for oneself as a human being who suffers or is in difficulty. It is not about making excuses, and, unlike feeling sorry for oneself, it doesn't undermine efforts to change things for the better. In fact, genuine self-empathy can be the starting point for tackling problems, changing unwanted behaviors, and coping with difficult circumstances that cannot be changed.

Opposed to self-empathy, and often standing in its way, is the inner critic, the part of us that makes negative judgments about ourselves. Often it comes as a voice inside saying, "You're being stupid," "I'm not good enough," "You're ugly," "I'll get in trouble," "I'm a bad person." (Mine usually just says, "You idiot!"—often right out loud before I can catch myself.) The inner critic causes us to doubt ourselves, to avoid doing things we want to do, or to feel shame or guilt about things we did do (it is related to Freud's concept of the superego). Critic attacks can be blatant or subtle. They can shout in your ear ("You idiot!"), or they can be just a whisper from the shadows ("I better be careful" or "I ought to be doing something else right now").

It is difficult, perhaps impossible, to get rid of the inner critic entirely. Nor would we want to: as judgmental and unfriendly as it can be, it contains its own form of intelligence and is a potential ally if we learn how to make the right relationship with it. The key to responding constructively to the inner critic is to begin by noticing and *acknowledging* it when it shows up. Usually we feel victimized by the critic's negativity and either become deflated ("Yeah, I'll never be able to do it right, so why bother?") or get into a struggle with it ("No, I'm not being lazy; it's just that I don't feel well right now!"). Both of these are reactive and ultimately self-defeating. The key to *responding* rather than reacting is, first of all, to recognize the inner critic for what it is and get some distance from it. Don't accept its authoritarian voice at face value. Like the Wizard of Oz, behind its façade of superiority and power, the inner critic is in reality timid and ineffectual. Recognize it as only a particular voice or part or place in you, certainly not all of you, and don't submit to its pronouncements or try to fight back.

Here are three strategies for dealing with the inner critic:

Acknowledge and dismiss. Much of the time this is the simplest way of defusing negative self-judgments. First recognize that the inner critic has appeared on the scene: "Oh, there you are again, always criticizing!" Then, having identified it, dismiss it. You can do the dismissing by simply ignoring it after you've recognized it, or by saying something to it like, "I don't have time for you right now," "I'm not listening," "I'm not afraid of you," or by imagining that you are actually pushing it out of your way.

Acknowledge and reframe. This approach begins in the same way—"Oh, there you are again" (or "there it is again")—but instead of dismissing the critic out of hand, you take time to see what intelligence its criticism contains. The reframing is to ignore the unsympathetic messenger but consider the source of the message. Perhaps there is an aspect of your situation that isn't sitting right with you, and the critic's intervention alerts you to identify what it is and modify your approach.

Acknowledge and befriend.* This is the most radical option. You won't have time to do it every time the critic shows up, but when you can, it is possible to turn your seeming enemy into a real ally. Underneath its harsh, judgmental tone, the critic is usually trying to protect you in some way, like a frantic mother screaming at her child: "Get away from that stove, stupid!" The tone is angry or belittling, but its source is the mother's fierce need to protect her child from harm.

Befriending the critic is like inviting someone you're in conflict with to take a time-out and talk things through. To do this, you have to suspend your own agenda long enough to really listen to what's bothering the other person and appreciate how things appear from their perspective.

Here's how such an exchange with the inner critic might go. Note that the self—your current, grown-up self—listens to exactly what the inner critic says and reflects it back with empathy before going on.

INNER CRITIC (IC): That's a stupid idea.

SELF: I hear that you think this might not be such a good idea. What are you worried could happen?

---

* This way of working with the inner critic is based on the pioneering work of Ann Weiser Cornell and Barbara McGavin in Inner Relationship Focusing.

IC: You'll make a total fool of yourself.

SELF: OK, I hear you. You're really worried that I'll make a fool of myself. And could you tell me what you're afraid would happen then?

IC: *(After a pause during which you wait patiently with interested attention)* You'd lose your friends.

SELF: Oh, you're really worried that I might lose all my friends if I make a mistake and make a fool of myself. Yes, I get it, that's certainly something one would worry about. . . . Can you say what would be the worst thing about losing all my friends? *(Though the answer to such a question may seem self-evident, it is important to hear exactly how the critic expresses it.)*

IC: You would be left all alone, no one would support you, you'd just shrivel up and die . . . *(The inner critic tends to exaggerate. Don't react; just keep listening and responding sympathetically, as you would with an upset child.)*

SELF: Of course, you're really scared that I might end up abandoned by my friends and feeling all alone. Is that it?

IC: Yes, that's it. *(The inner critic feels heard. With this affirmation from the self, it no longer needs to criticize and be negative. It is ready be on your side. Now's the time to inquire for the positive energy it has been concealing all along.)*

SELF: And can you let me know what you're wanting?

IC: I want [or I want you] to feel liked and respected and supported by other people.

SELF: You want to feel liked, respected, and supported by others. Yes, those are things that I really value and feel good about. *(The self receives the positive wanting that has emerged in the dialogue, taking it in and savoring it. The critic has turned into an ally, and the energy it has been holding can now reintegrate with the whole self.)*

This example is, of course, somewhat idealized. The critic might have more fears to express before it feels completely heard.

Or it could dig in its heels and refuse to talk at all. Then there is further exploration to do, perhaps at a later date and, in the case of long-standing issues, over the course of many sessions. Remember, *you* (the self) can't force the inner critical place to relax. Sometimes the best we can do is "agree to disagree" and move ahead knowing the inner critic isn't completely assuaged, yet not letting it stand in our way.

Addressing a felt sense or a part as "you," as if you are talking to another person, works better for some people than others. Because it helps provide a safe distance, it is especially helpful for those who tend to collapse into or become overwhelmed by emotions. For those who are more distant from their emotions to begin with, it may work better to bring the part closer: "There's *a part of me* that is feeling afraid of appearing stupid to other people." If even "a part of me" feels too distant, try to really own the feeling by identifying with it—"*I* am feeling afraid of . . ."— and then check if this statement rings true to your felt sense. Once you have owned the feeling in this way, you can still recognize that it is not *all* of you; there are other more positive aspects too.

In the following exercise I suggest some basic steps in befriending the critic. These are intended as guideposts only. Don't feel constrained by them; trust your own inner process. If you find yourself going off into discursive thinking or fantasy, bring yourself back to how things feel in your body. If the going gets rough, remember that self-empathy is your secret weapon for returning to grounded aware presence whenever you feel menaced by too much fear, anger, confusion, or painful emotions like shame and guilt.

Exercise 9.2 Befriending the Inner Critic

Think of a place or voice in you that is frequently self-critical: "I'm lazy/undisciplined/fat/stupid." It can be a recurring theme or something triggered by a specific incident. Start with acknowledging: "I'm noticing a part of me [a voice, a place, something in me] that says I'm stupid [unattractive, weak, etc.]." Invite this inner place or voice to be present. Keeping enough distance to feel safe, regard it with respect and appreciation, even if it appears ugly or threatening. Know that your larger self is in charge and can choose to back away or dismiss the critical place if you start to feel panicky or overwhelmed.

As you become comfortable being with this place, help it to get comfortable too: "Yes, I see you there. I'm not trying to get rid of you; I really want to hear what you have to say." Just be with it, keeping it company for a while. When it feels right, ask it gently what it's afraid of, what it's not wanting to have happen. Listen empathically and receive what it has to say, even if you know it is exaggerated or untrue. Reflect it back: "I understand, you're worried that . . ." Continue this back and forth until the critic, which by now may have become more of a scared, vulnerable place, feels fully heard. Then, ask it what it needs or wants, what would allow it to feel better and relax its vigilance. Again, go back and forth until it feels fully heard and acknowledged. Then you can also ask it, "What are you wanting for me?" Having been recognized and respected, the critic can contribute its positive wanting for you, helping you to acknowledge and embrace suppressed needs for love, recognition, respect, strength, desire, confidence, and so on. End by thanking the inner-critic-turned-ally and let whatever positive, fresh insight and energy have come permeate your whole being. Feel filled with it, as you might feel after a nourishing meal.

I want to repeat that the exercise instructions above represent a simplified, ideal version of what you are likely to experience when you first attempt to befriend the critic in yourself. I don't want to set you up to feel like a failure if you don't get to that nourishing-meal feeling! Feelings of failure or frustration, by the way, are another occasion for the vital resource of self-empathy. When things aren't going well, when it feels too hard or too confusing or just plain unproductive, self-empathy is especially called for. We need to learn to soothe ourselves, to say, "You know, this is hard, I'm really struggling here"—as a caring parent might soothe a struggling child.

In the process of listening to and receiving the critic's fears and wants, you may sometimes need to revisit painful experiences. Because of the ability to center yourself in grounded aware presence and adopt the attitude of friendly attending, you now have the possibility of reexperiencing the painful feelings from a safe distance and with self-empathy. This can be a deeply healing process. Remember, however, that when you are dealing with complex trauma rooted in overwhelming threats to survival or personal integrity, a skilled therapist or counselor is often needed to facilitate the process and guard against retraumatization.

The following exercise is presented as a brief indication of how the skills you are cultivating through Mindful Focusing can be brought to bear in working with difficult past experiences. It is optional. If at any point painful emotions evoked by this exercise threaten to overwhelm you, stop. Don't go beyond what feels safe for you. By keeping within your present threshold of tolerance, you can become comfortable over time in staying present with more painful or threatening material.

Exercise 9.3   Reexperiencing Painful Feelings

Recall a time, perhaps during childhood, when you experienced hurt, fear, grief, shame, or regret. Let the felt sense of that time come in your body—enough that you experience its discomfort but at a safe distance from which you can also feel self-empathy.

From the larger, compassionate you, feel empathy for the suffering you. You can say to yourself, "That's a very difficult thing for anyone to experience; I feel real compassion and caring for the one who had to go through that." Feeling old pain and making a new relationship with it is a way of welcoming an abandoned part back into the family, inviting its locked-up energy to open and contribute to the good of the whole.

When we experience anger, guilt, shame, and other negative emotions, by honestly acknowledging their presence in us *but not collapsing into them,* we can find compassion for ourselves. Even when we feel alone and without comfort in our own suffering, we can appreciate that this is what other human beings in all times and places have also experienced. Enlarging our sense of compassion to include others' suffering makes it easier to be friendly to our own.

Interlude

THE NEXT TWO CHAPTERS are an invitation to pause and reflect on some of the sources of the inner skills you have been cultivating. We'll take a break from guided exercises to look briefly
at two principal thought systems, one Eastern and one Western,
which inform Mindful Focusing. The meeting and mixing of
historically separate world wisdom traditions in our times is an
exciting development, one that can contribute to mutual respect
and collaboration across cultures. Mindful Focusing represents
one way of actualizing this cross-fertilization.

Chapter 10 presents a brief overview of Mindful Focusing's
sources in mindfulness-awareness meditation and the mandala
principle as they have been passed down through many centuries of Buddhist tradition. Chapter 11 looks at Eugene Gendlin's
Philosophy of the Implicit, a deep investigation into the nature of
life processes that extends Western philosophy and psychology by
articulating the centrality of the felt-sensing capacity to human
development.

Part 2, "Living Life Forward," draws on some of the theoreti-
cal discussion in these chapters. Theory sparks our understanding
and can be a real aid to learning inner skills. That said, knowing
the theory is not essential to mastering the skills. If the material

in these chapters seems like a distraction or an obstacle rather than a support, feel free to skip forward and start working with the exercises in part 2. You can come back to the concepts presented here if and when you feel it helpful.

Chapter 10

Mindfulness, Awareness, and the Sovereign Self

THE "MINDFUL" PART of Mindful Focusing derives from the Buddhist meditation tradition. The first exercise in this book— Grounded Aware Presence, or GAP—has its roots in my own years of practice and study with the Tibetan teacher Chögyam Trungpa Rinpoche. In this chapter, we will explore some of the principles behind grounded aware presence.

Mindfulness

Following in the footsteps of Eastern mind-body practices like judo, karate, and hatha yoga that became popular in the West during the twentieth century, Asian-derived techniques for developing mindfulness are now becoming known and practiced globally as we enter the twenty-first century. In part this phenomenon is driven by extraordinary developments in the field of cognitive neuroscience. With the advent of functional magnetic resonance imaging (fMRI) and other new technologies for exploring the brain in real time, scientific evidence for the efficacy of these practices is accumulating rapidly. *The Mindful Brain* and *Mindsight* by Daniel Siegel, M.D., are two excellent examples of recent books describing and interpreting the newly emerging understanding of how the brain and nervous system function and the ways in which mindfulness-awareness practices can enhance their functioning.

In colloquial usage, *mindfulness* means paying attention, staying focused on a task, not getting distracted. In the context of meditation, or mindfulness practice, it denotes a particular quality of moment-to-moment attention. Jon Kabat-Zinn, the leading proponent of mindfulness in health care, defines it as "paying attention in a particular way: on purpose, in the present moment, and nonjudgmentally."[1]

Mindfulness practice involves periods of sitting still and training one's mind to stay on a particular object, typically one's own breathing. When thoughts, sensations, memories, emotions, and so forth arise in the mind, as they inevitably will, the practice is simply to make note of them without judgment and return one's attention to the breath. As the practitioner does this over a period of days, weeks, and more, the mind's natural tendency to become engrossed in a particular subject, or to jump impulsively from one object of attention to another, gradually subsides. The mind becomes unusually calm, at first intermittently but with regular practice in a more sustained way. At the same time, it becomes clearer, like muddy water that settles when left undisturbed. Mental contents are perceived more accurately, and concentration improves.

An important component of mindfulness is body awareness, really noticing the different parts, movements, and textures of our physical bodies and experiencing them from the inside. The first step in GAP, *grounded,* refers to the body's earthiness, its substance and weight, and its felt connection to the external world as it rests on the earth anchored and supported by the force of gravity. Being grounded is the experiential foundation for feelings of stability, balance, ease, and uprightness.

Awareness

The kind of mindfulness that is cultivated in Buddhist medita-tion is frequently referred to as mindfulness-awareness or mind-ful awareness. Whereas the word *mindfulness* suggests the element of effort involved in deliberately placing and sustaining attention on a chosen object, *awareness* has more to do with the quality of consciousness itself.

Although awareness is present whenever we are conscious, there can be awareness with no mindfulness, as in the experience of driving a car "on automatic." Even though we don't notice what we're doing—turning the wheel on a curve, stepping on the brakes at a red light—clearly some awareness is operating. We may not be able to recollect these actions after the fact, but in the moment our awareness functions quite precisely.

At the next level there is ordinary mindful awareness, deliber-ately paying attention to a particular object or situation. When we drive mindfully, we pay attention to the road conditions, traf-fic, and our route; our minds are on the job.

Then there is a further level, known as meta-awareness, in which we are *aware that we are aware.* This doubled awareness enhances mental clarity and gives rise to more vivid perceptions and penetrating insights into the true nature of things. Even beyond that is a kind of meta-meta-awareness, or "panoramic awareness," that is like a vast open space of consciousness in which endless thoughts, perceptions, emotions, and sensations keep appearing and disappearing while the space itself remains continuous and ever present.

Imagine you are reading this book while flying in an air-plane. If your mind wanders, you may still be following the words, but you're not really getting the meaning: this would be the level of automatic awareness without mindfulness. If you are absorbed in the book, taking in the meaning of the words, you are in a state of ordinary mindful awareness: your attention is focused on the matter at hand. Beyond that, you can notice the fact that you are reading the book as you read it: now you are being self-aware, or meta-aware, of the activity of reading. You could also be aware that you are reading the book while seated in an airplane. Expanding awareness even further, you can have all those levels *plus* the realization that "me-reading-a-book-while-sitting-here-in-an-airplane" is itself moving through the vast open space of the sky. This is an experience of panoramic awareness—big mind that can accommodate anything. Like the blue sky, it is open, clear, and undisturbed: occasional birds or puffs of cloud may be vividly seen, but they don't interrupt the vastness of the sky. The second step of GAP, *awareness*, aims to open us to this deeper, more panoramic level of consciousness.

Mindfulness-awareness meditation cultivates these three levels of awareness: clear concentration, self-aware situational insight, and panoramic awareness. Over time the three become integrated into a strong, supple, alive-in-the-moment quality of ongoing consciousness. As Chögyam Trungpa Rinpoche put it: "[One is] not living in the future but living in the present. The present situation is open—you could almost say solid—and real, definite, and healthy. There is an appreciation of the richness in the present."[2]

"Living in the present" brings us to the third step of GAP. *Presence* is a sense of basic existence, mindfully and awarely being who you are right here and right now. When you experience the quality of presence, you are simply here, at this moment, being present—in yourself and to yourself. Ideally, this is an experience of utter simplicity. At the same time, it raises a central question: Who is the one who is being present? Who is being mindful, being aware? Who is doing or having these experiences? Who are you?

The Sovereign Self

Who am I? is an enormous question that has engaged and baffled theologians, philosophers, psychologists, and ordinary people for thousands of years. René Descartes asserted proof of his own existence with the famous formula "I think, therefore I am." The Buddha, on the other hand, taught *anatman*, nonself—the insubstantiality of what we call I. Fortunately, for the purposes of this book, we don't need to worry about the philosophical or existential status of the I; rather, we are interested in the lived experiences that are being referenced when we use the word *I*.

We can think of "I" or "myself" as the central source of our thoughts, feelings, and perceptions. It is "where we're coming from." However, if we examine our experience carefully and candidly, we notice that where we're coming from can be very different at different times. The "self" we are operating from at any given time is more like a partial self, a certain version of "me" that shows up in response to a particular set of circumstances. In the case of multiple personality disorder, these different *I*'s can manifest as totally separate personalities. Most of us don't evidence such an extreme of inner disconnectedness, but all of us show up in different ways at different times, and all of us experience inner conflicts: "Part of me wants to go out, but another part of me wants to stay home."

A healthy, whole, centered self is able to recognize and coordinate the functioning of the many partial selves. A helpful way of visualizing this is by means of the mandala, the circular structure that appears in different forms in many world wisdom traditions. In Tibetan Buddhism, a typical mandala depicts a deity as a sovereign king or queen seated at the center of a palace in the center of a walled city at the center of the world. Surrounding the central figure are the different halls and courtyards of the palace, then a series of neighborhoods where the subjects of the kingdom reside, then the countryside, mountain chains, and finally the ocean. From his or her throne at the center of the mandala, the sovereign surveys the whole of existence and empowers and protects all of the subjects so they can perform their different roles in society. The sovereign, who is understood to be a genuinely enlightened leader, embodies qualities of vision, authority, responsibility, beneficence, and skillful action.

Likewise, each of us possesses an inner sovereign, a sovereign *I*, capable of manifesting these same positive qualities. When we are being our sovereign *I*, it is like occupying a throne that sits at the center of our self, our life, and our world. We are in a state of grounded aware presence that is in touch with and responsive to our total environment.

Chögyam Trungpa Rinpoche wrote a poem called "You Might Be Tired of the Seat That You Deserve." We each *deserve* to manifest as our sovereign self, to occupy our central being, but doing so takes courage, self-awareness, self-mastery, and self-empathy. As we cultivate our felt sense as a vital inner resource, we are at the same time strengthening the sovereign *I* as our central seat of awareness and response-ability. This inner sovereign is both the seat of our consciousness and the source of right action—actions that feel wholly and deeply right. As you use the exercises in this book to cultivate your capacity for self-awareness, self-empathy, and personal growth, you are also developing your sovereign *I*, your capacity to act in the world with clarity, confidence, accountability, caring, and skill.

Chapter 11

The Deep Nature of
Life Process

We hear so much about the accelerating rate of change in virtually all aspects of life in the twenty-first century. Here's *New York Times* columnist Tom Friedman advising President Obama at the beginning of his second term in 2013:

> Obama needs to explain to Americans the world in which they're now living. It's a world in which the increasing velocity of globalization and the Information Technology revolution are reshaping every job, workplace and industry. As a result, the mantra that if you "just work hard and play by the rules" you should expect a middle-class lifestyle is no longer operable. Today you need to work harder and smarter, learn and relearn faster and longer to be in the middle class.

Along with this external imperative to change that Friedman describes, as individuals we feel an internal imperative of personal change as the key to achieving and sustaining good health, satisfying relationships, and a sense of fulfillment in life. But why this never-ending drumbeat of change, change, change? What's wrong with staying the same?

The Paradox of Change

From one point of view, nothing at all is wrong with staying the same. Indeed, staying the same is the key to our survival: to go on living, we need to maintain the integrity of our body and its ongoing processes like respiration, circulation, and digestion, which need to keep doing the same things, over and over and over. However, when we look more closely, we see that each of these life processes itself consists of continual change. Breathing is inhaling—changing to exhaling. Circulation is oxygenated blood pumping from the lungs to every part of the body—changing to deoxygenated blood returning through the veins and the heart back to the lungs to expel carbon dioxide and pick up a fresh load of oxygen. Eating is taking in food, chewing, and digesting—changing to absorption of nutrients through the gut and elimination of waste.

Each iteration of breathing, blood circulation, and eating is functionally "the same"—it serves the same basic purpose—and yet no two cycles are identical. Each time, the pattern is subtly changed by the particulars of the moment, both externally and internally. And, of course, all the different body processes are inter-affecting one another. In other words, each life process is a pattern of change that itself is being changed from moment to moment. A rock can just sit there for centuries doing nothing, but a living thing must be continuously changing if it is to survive. As William Butler Yeats wrote in his great poem "Easter 1916":

> The horse that comes from the road,
> The rider, the birds that range
> From cloud to tumbling cloud,
> Minute by minute they change. . . .

Hence the beautiful paradox of life: living things must change in order to stay the same. Or, more precisely, living things must change in order to stay *themselves*. Biologists Humberto Maturana and Francisco Varela introduced the theory of autopoiesis, a Greek-derived term that simply means "self-making." Life is the ongoing process of self-making. It is that which continuously changes itself in order to continue being itself.

Interaction First

Now let's go a little deeper, with Eugene Gendlin as our guide. Like Maturana and Varela, Gendlin understands living beings as processes rather than things. A core concept in his Philosophy of the Implicit is what he calls "interaction first." Any living thing, from a virus to a human, is first and foremost an ongoing interactive process in and with its environment. Although we commonly think of animals and plants as autonomous units that interact with a preexisting environment, Gendlin is saying that the reverse is true. Life is a single, integrated process that generates both the living thing and its environment. This doesn't mean there is no external environment independent of ourselves—we know that life is only a very recent development in the history of the universe—but it means that the environment *as we experience it* is a product of our particular kind of life process. Dogs have evolved to hear high-pitched sounds that are inaudible to us; migrating birds navigate by Earth's magnetic field in ways unavailable to the human organism, and so on.

"Interaction first" also means that in our relationships with others, in some odd way the relationship is "prior" to the individuals having the relationship. How is this possible? Common sense tells us that when we meet a new person, each of us has already been around as ourselves for many years, whereas the relationship is only just beginning. But if we examine our actual experience precisely, we discover that how we show up in any particular relationship is determined—created, really—by what the other person brings out in us. It is like a chemical interaction—hydrogen and oxygen are both invisible gases, yet together they make water, a visible, touchable, tastable liquid that seems to have nothing in common with the two elements that formed it. Human beings are not transformed quite so radically in relationships (though at certain special times it can feel that way), but who and what we are is always a function of who and what we are interacting with. Like it or not, we live by changing/being changed by our ever-unfolding interactions.

Carrying Forward

Our basic needs for oxygen, food, warmth, safety, connectedness, love, and so forth are functions of our nature as living things. But, Gendlin stresses, the ways in which these needs get met are not predetermined. What we call a "need" is better thought of as a particular life process that implies a certain *direction* of change. The potential ways to move in that direction, the possible next steps available to the organism, are infinite. When something occurs in an organism's environment that "meets" the implied direction of change, the life process is able to move ahead. In Gendlin's language, it "carries forward." If nothing in the environment meets the implied direction, the need remains unmet and is held in the body as a "stopped process."

We saw earlier that a living thing must continuously change in order to stay the same, to keep being itself. When a process is stopped, it can no longer go through its implied changes and therefore is unable to sustain its integrity, which is to say its health and well-being. Some stoppages are fatal—if we can't breathe or circulate blood, we die in a matter of minutes. If we can't find food, the process takes longer but the result will be the same. However, many stoppages are not fatal. They cause some measure of dysfunction, but the organism is able to live on, growing beyond or around the stoppage. Sometimes the dysfunction can be solved by other means. An artificial limb would be an example: a leg that has been lost can't be restored, but a prosthesis can allow the functional process called *walking* to resume.

A particularly dramatic instance of a stopped process getting carried forward by novel means shows up in the approach to treating phantom limb syndrome developed by V. S. Ramachandran at the University of California, San Diego. People who have lost a limb often continue to have sensations as if the limb were still present. Ramachandran had one such patient, Philip, who experienced a painful paralysis in his missing left arm, which he had lost in an accident many years earlier. Ramachandran constructed a simple box divided in half by a mirror, open at the top and with armholes in the front on either side of the mirror. As Ramachandran describes it:

> I asked Philip to place his right hand on the right side of the mirror in the box and imagine that his left hand (the phantom) was on the left side. "I want you to move your right and left arm simultaneously," I instructed.
>
> "Oh, I can't do that," said Philip. "I can move my right arm, but my left arm is frozen. Every morning when I get up, I try to move my phantom because it's in this funny position and I feel that moving it might help relieve the pain. But," he said, looking down at his invisible arm, "I never have been able to generate a flicker of movement in it."
>
> "Okay, Philip, but try anyway."
>
> Philip rotated his body, shifting his shoulder, to "insert" his lifeless phantom into the box. Then he put his right hand on the other side of the mirror and attempted to make synchronous movements. As he gazed into the mirror, he gasped and then cried out, "Oh, my God! Oh, my God, doctor! This is unbelievable. It's mind-boggling!" He was jumping up and down like a kid. "My left arm is plugged in again. It's as if I'm in the past. All these memories from years ago are flooding

back into my mind. I can move my arm again. I can feel my elbow moving, my wrist moving. It's all moving again." [1]

The mirror created a perfect illusion that his left arm was moving in the same way that his right arm was, providing feedback to Philip's brain that unblocked the painful, paralyzed sensation and allowed him to reexperience movement in the arm, together with associated memories and feelings from childhood! Because his *whole* body process still implied a living left arm, the illusion provided by the mirror allowed Philip's brain, in effect, to update itself. The frozen neural circuitry, the physiological expression of the stopped process, suddenly released, and the arm came alive again, albeit virtually, in the present.

In this remarkable anecdote, no amount of conscious effort on Philip's part made any difference; his brain had to be tricked into resetting itself. However, Eugene Gendlin's great contribution has been to identify an exact but subtle method whereby many kinds of stopped process can be recognized and released through a special kind of conscious effort. Gendlin challenged the received Freudian paradigm of the unconscious as some kind of hidden operating system haunted by psychic monsters. He replaced it with a new paradigm in which all the unseen "drives" that had been relegated to the unconscious are recognized as the *living body* itself.

The body *embodies* and *is* all of the implied directions involved in surviving and thriving as a living organism. For Gendlin, these implied directions are not hidden somewhere else; they are always *implicitly* present in our moment-to-moment experience. Because they are implicit rather than explicit or manifest, they are not recognizable objects of awareness in the usual sense. But this doesn't mean that they are completely invisible or unexperienceable. They are present and accessible to experience at a level below the radar of ordinary, conscious awareness.

Philosophically as well as physiologically, all the things that constitute our ordinary awareness of reality—sense perceptions, thoughts, emotions—are virtual creations of our biology. Recent neuroscience is shedding light on this virtualness, or insubstantiality of conscious experience (and confirming much of what Buddhism and other wisdom traditions have taught for thousands of years). Our experience of the world is almost entirely indirect.

Paradoxically, however, the unmanifested, not-yet-patterned, implicit level of lived experience is *direct*. It is our ongoing life process itself, which, though subtle, can be experienced as the unclear yet palpable felt texture of being alive in any particular moment. In his philosophical work, Gendlin calls this the "direct referent." Practically speaking, it is synonymous with the felt sense.

Felt-sensing, or Focusing as Gendlin named it, is a learnable ability to bring bodily stopped processes into awareness and interact with them. Note that the word *stopped* here is positive as well as negative because it refers to a process that, although it is not actually happening, continues to be *implied*. The right direction for the organism to take is still present as a kind of nonconceptual, not-yet-clear wanting/knowing of the sort of object or behavior that would allow the life process to resume. Any stopped process, although unable to move ahead right now, continues to imply the endless possible ways that it *could* carry forward, including ways that have never existed before.

Focusing is a technique specifically designed for bringing the implied life direction into awareness, in the (formless) form of the felt sense, so that our higher human capacities for making sense of things can function with its guidance. What makes felt-sensing so powerful, and so important in our continued survival as a species, is its ability to connect evolutionarily different levels of life process. It is a new human capacity, appearing at this very challenging point in history, to get our reptilian, mammalian, and human parts to talk to one another and work in closer alignment.

Part Two

Living Life Forward

Chapter *12*

From Insights to
Action Steps

THE FIRST HALF of this book was devoted to a series of exercises designed to build the basic skill set for finding your felt sense. In the previous two chapters, we took a brief look at some of the theory underlying Mindful Focusing, adding the key concepts of the sovereign self and carrying forward. Now we are ready to look at practical applications in specific areas of everyday life.

The felt sense is most fruitful when it generates insights and action steps that move us toward our goals in alignment with our deepest values. How can you translate the information and inspiration you receive from the felt sense into concrete steps to take in your relationships, work situations, and other aspects of life?

I am writing this chapter while in retreat in the Colorado Rockies. Shambhala Mountain Center, where I am staying for a week of meditation and writing, lies in a beautiful high meadow dotted with rugged ponderosa pine trees surrounded by forested hills and craggy rock peaks. I first set foot here forty years ago as a young student of Buddhism. I feel a combination of nostalgia and fresh wonder to be once again in this magical place.

But I have a problem. The rough drafts for two chapters that

I intended to work on while in retreat are nowhere to be found. I clearly remember e-mailing them to myself before leaving home. As I think this, I feel a twinge in my chest that is saying something like, "You technological klutz! Obviously you did something wrong. Plus, you should have confirmed that the files got transmitted before you left." Ah, my inner critic has put in an appearance!

Giving it friendly attending, I hear that the critic has more to say: "You're never going to really succeed because you always mess up one way or another. You are helpless on your own!" Instead of getting defensive, I welcome the twinge and the critic into my awareness. Soon I sense a more vulnerable place that conveys the feeling "I seem to always make these kinds of mistakes. Now I've come all this way and I can't do the work I intended to do in this special place." With that, the twinge softens into a palpable sense of sadness and disappointment. Now, in place of self-denigration ("You klutz!"), I am able to feel some self-compassion, something like "Yes, I do tend to get things like this wrong, and yes, of course, it is very frustrating."

I give this critical place some (self-) empathy. I inquire as gently as I can:

SELF: What are you worrying about? What is the worst part of this?

INNER CRITIC: Not being able to measure up.

SELF: And what would it feel like in the body if you did measure up?

IC: Shiny, self-authoring, able to play with friends and colleagues whom I admire. Able to contribute and be recognized. Able to move on to the next thing.

Now I sense a sadness inside that comes with the thought "This is so familiar." A soft ache extends from my throat down to my belly.

Given this seeming impasse, what can I do now to use my time here productively? I need to find an action step.* The first thing that comes to mind is to e-mail my wife and ask her to send the missing files. But this doesn't sit quite right—she is very busy with her own work, and it will be difficult for her to locate the files on my computer at home.

I remember that I do have with me an overview of the book prepared for the publisher that includes a table of contents with brief descriptions of all of the chapters. Perhaps, instead of using this time to finish the chapters I already have in draft form, I can skip ahead to ones I haven't worked on yet. I sit with this possibility for a few moments, checking it against my felt sense. Is there anything in the way of skipping over the chapters I'd intended to work on? Although I still sense a slight pang of disappointment, I also see that the new chapters don't depend on having everything ahead of them finished. It will work just as well to resume work on the earlier ones upon my return home. Yes, it feels OK to shift course and go directly to the later chapters.

In fact, now I see that I have had some anxiety about the second half of the book, worry that I won't have as much to say or that I'll have trouble coming up with appropriate exercises. But here I am in this glorious, fresh place, and now I will move into fresh territory with my writing. My action step is—to write the chapter about action steps! This feels just right, and along with this sense of rightness comes a surge of fresh energy.

This real-time example of finding an action step may seem unremarkable: skipping ahead to work on new chapters seems an obvious enough solution to my dilemma. But it wasn't at all obvious to me before I took the time to visit with my felt sense. All I felt was frustration at not being able to do what I'd planned to, plus incompetence at having failed to send the draft copies. If

---

* It would be more accurate to say, "I want to and I choose to . . ." I could have chosen to stay with the "soft ache" longer, or with the "shiny, self-authoring." Focusing is an active process that includes making choices about what we spend time with.

I hadn't taken the time for some Mindful Focusing, I most likely would have ended up calling my wife, interrupting her work, trying to explain where to find the files, and so on. Perhaps it would have worked out in the end, or perhaps it would have wasted a bunch of time for us both. In either case, I would have missed the *implicit* opportunity to connect with my deeper feelings about being back in this special place in the Colorado mountains, and the fresh perspective and energy it held for tackling the second half of the book.

Note that in order to move ahead, I had to both find the new action step and let go of my attachment to the original plan. *Attachment* is a revealing word here, highlighting that our intentions in life are as much physical as they are mental. My body needed some attention paid to what it was already attached to in order to let go of that and move in a different direction. Consulting my felt sense allowed the energy I had invested in the old intention to shift toward the new step that came for me.

Exercise 12.1   Finding a Right Next Step

Bring awareness inside. Think of a few situations in your life that are waiting for a next step from you. Contemplate each situation briefly, then let your felt sense help you decide on one to go into more deeply—perhaps the most immediate or the one where you feel most stuck.

Take enough time to review the aspects of that situation in more detail, letting a felt sense of the whole of it form. When you feel ready, ask gently inside:

- What's in the way of my making progress here?
- What is this situation needing or wanting now?
- What would be a right next step?

As possible next steps come to mind, check them against the felt sense of the whole situation. Do they fit? Do they leave any aspect of the situation unmet? Is there anything in the way of your taking this action as the next step? Does the step feel right in your body; does it bring fresh energy and inspiration?

Be careful about action steps that are too ambitious— New Year's resolutions like "I'm going to lose thirty pounds" or "I'm going to exercise for an hour every morning." These are setups for failure. Find a next step that moves you in the direction of your goals but is also doable. Guidelines for "doable" are:

Is the proposed step specific?
Can I visualize clearly when, where, and how it will happen?
Can it be completed in the near future? (If it can't be done within the next week or two, look for a smaller, intermediate step that can.)

Finally, form an inner intention to take the action step. See yourself actually doing it, resonate with your felt sense a final time for a feeling of rightness, and commit to doing it.

Often the key to success is in finding small steps. By biting off no more than you can chew, you increase your chances of success—and build momentum for further steps. But don't be afraid to stretch yourself. Some action steps are straightforward and easy to accomplish, but often a next step that comes from your felt sense will move you out of your comfort zone. It feels different from the way you have done things in the past. These kinds of challenges are exciting: you are taking action to affect the external situation, and you are changing *yourself* in the process. These are steps of real personal growth.

Chapter 13

Deep Listening

From finding right action steps to live our lives forward in the world, we move now to the all-important topic of living forward our *relationships* with other people.

In relationships we locate ourselves, deepen our experience of what it is to be human, discover our own hearts, find our true center. And—relationships challenge us, pull us off center, muddy the water, bring us down from airy heaven to rugged earth. (I've heard marriage defined as a lengthy journey to discover who you really are—while fending off someone only too eager to tell you!) Relationships that are alive and growing are periodically stressed, strained, and ruptured in ways small or large by the emerging, changing needs and behaviors of the different individuals involved.

Real relationships must be built and renewed through repeated cycles of rupture and repair. During rupture we are thrown back on ourselves, compelled to recognize our own neediness and shortcomings. We are faced with the choice of feeling like victims and seeing the other as selfish and hurtful, or recognizing our own needs more clearly and, also, the differing needs of a separate, unique human being. This calls for a kind of bifocal empathy—nearsighted empathy for ourselves and farsighted empathy for others. This double empathy lays the foundation for repair. Actually, *reattunement* is a better word here than *repair*. Unlike a car that's been repaired, the reattuned relationship won't operate the same as before. Rather, something will have transformed, the human bond grown deeper, stronger, more caring, less self-protective.

Relationship and the Evolving Self

We are each unique. Yet we become our unique selves only *in relationship* with others. An infant, whose experience of being alive in the world begins with no split between self and other, no "me" and "you" and "it," has to learn to differentiate itself as a separate individual. At the center of this process is the relationship between the infant and its primary caregiver. By the way Mother attunes to Baby, responding to cries with feeding, to looks with smiles, to distress with hugs, to gestures and sounds with mirroring movements and verbalizations, the young child gradually builds an inner model of itself as a separate individual interacting with others and the world. During the early years of life, children learn both to differentiate themselves—think of the "terrible twos"—and to harmonize or attune their behavior with others'.

This process of differentiation and attunement does not end in childhood. It continues throughout the life span, into old age and even the dying process. It creates a rhythm of rupture and reattunement that is central to our relationships and their change over time. Ruptures are inevitable, but reattunement is a skill that can be cultivated. According to developmental psychologist Daniel Siegel:

> When we attune to others we allow our own internal state to shift, to come to resonate with the inner world of another. This resonance is at the heart of the important sense of "feeling felt" that emerges in close relationships. Children need

attunement to feel secure and to develop well, and throughout our lives we need attunement to feel close and connected.[1]

At times of rupture, it is hard to hold self-empathy and other-
empathy together. The good news is that cultivating the capacity
for self-empathy, as you have been doing in the various exercises
up to this point, strengthens your ability to sustain empathy for
others. As Martin Luther King, Jr., succinctly put it, "the right
kind of self-love and the right kind of love of others are inter-
dependent."[2]

Deep Listening

What distinguishes humans from other life forms is our use of
complex symbolic communication in carrying forward the activities that constitute our lives. Although interpersonal attunement originates and is most immediate in direct body-to-body
contact—parent with child and, later, lover with lover—verbal
exchanges dominate in most of our lives. Accordingly, the central
factor in attuning to others is our capacity for listening.

Deep listening means to listen *from* a deeper place in oneself
to a deeper place in others. Centered in our own grounded aware
presence, we are able to extend friendly attending to others, cata-
lyzing their ability to find their own felt sense by entering the
zone of their experience where confusion, vulnerability, and
other feelings usually kept in the shadows can show up. The primary catalyst is not asking questions or giving answers but the
palpable quality of our listening. Our simple human presence, of-
fered with no agenda of our own (not even to "help"), provides a
safe and empowering space for the other to go deep in themselves
and invite fresh knowing to come.

The best way to develop deep listening skills is by simply listening silently while another person shares thoughts and feelings
that are meaningful to them. I call this "just listening." For the

next exercise, you'll need to invite a friend or colleague to join you in a listening partnership—an exchange of turns during which one of you speaks and the other listens in silence. You can explain that you are not seeking any advice or feedback from them, just their friendly presence while you explore a topic and the feelings that it brings for you. During their turn, if your partner is not familiar with Focusing, you can suggest they use the time simply to "think out loud" about a problem or challenge in their life while you listen without commenting. This form of listening partnership is used extensively in the Focusing world, and the guideline is that the two partners agree in advance on how much time they want to spend and then divide it equally between them. Generally the Listener takes responsibility for keeping track of time and gives the Focuser (the speaking partner) a one-minute signal before their time is up.

One important caveat: Until both partners are skilled in deep listening, they should avoid sharing about situations that involve each other. This is to prevent the Listener, who is barred from responding, from becoming triggered by something the Focuser shares that has personal implications for them. Deep listening can become a powerful, transformational sharing between friends, colleagues, and intimate partners, but early on it is best to stick to topics that belong only to the person who is speaking. In the next chapter, we'll look at a modified version of this exercise that can be used to dialogue about issues of mutual concern.

Exercise 13.1   Just Listening

Sit comfortably close, facing each other so the Listener can take in nonverbal signals like breathing, posture, and body language. Decide who will speak first (the Focuser). Let your partner know that when you are the Listener, you will just listen without responding or asking questions at all, and that they are also welcome to pause and be silent at any point.

Agree that everything shared during the exchange will remain confidential. Confidentiality in this case means that the Listener not only won't repeat it to a third party, but won't bring it up with the Focuser afterward. This is important in helping people feel safe sharing about their personal issues. (If they decide to bring their issue up with you later on, then you are free to engage in normal conversation).

Agree on a specific length of time. I suggest starting with five minutes apiece and gradually extending that as you both become more comfortable with the process. It is the Listener's job to keep time and let the Focuser know when there is one minute remaining in their turn and, if needed, when their time is up.

Take time to come into grounded aware presence together— the more experienced partner can name the three steps of GAP, or you can just agree to start with a minute or so of silence. Then the Listener invites the Focuser to begin. When it is your turn to be Focuser, try keeping your eyes closed or lowered: this disrupts the habitual mode of "I'm telling you something" and encourages a more introspective mood.

After getting the one-minute signal, the Focuser should find a comfortable place to stop for now, understanding there may still be much more to explore in a later turn. The Focuser finishes their turn by thanking the Listener for listening and, when ready, inviting their partner to begin their turn as Focuser while they become the new, silent Listener.

In just listening, you refrain from any verbal response, including asking questions. This may feel unnatural at first, but it is valuable training for two reasons: it allows all your attention to go into empathic listening and, at the same time, alerts you to your own habitual tendencies to respond in certain ways. As you sustain your silence, you can take note of momentary impulses to ask a question, offer advice or comfort, or share something from your own experience. While wanting to help the other person is good in intention, at times we go about it in ways that are not helpful. Our impulses to problem-solve, express sympathy, or share similar experiences often have more to do with relieving uncomfortable feelings in ourselves than addressing the other person's actual needs. When we can internally acknowledge and allow space for our own emerging feelings without interrupting our partner, we make that same supportive space available for them to stay with their inner process. In a real-life interchange, such strict silence may not feel appropriate, but once you're comfortable with it, you'll find many times when such nonverbal, spacious listening is the best response.

Here are the Listener instructions in outline form for easy reference while practicing. The Focuser can refer to the Mindful Focusing Protocol guidelines on page 54.

Deep Listening Protocol

1. Grounded Aware Presence
   - center attention at your base, head, and heart (or)
   - settle your body, drop thinking, bring awareness inside your torso
2. Friendly Attending
   - listen to your partner but don't speak
   - double empathy—open, empathic, nonjudgmental, in touch with your own felt sense as you sense for the inner source from which the other person is speaking
   - note your own reactions as they arise
     - clarity/confusion
     - agreement/disagreement
     - pleasure/discomfort
     - wanting to help, solve, or fix

> accept your own reactions without self-judgment
> return to open, empathic, nonjudgmental listening to your partner

3. Keep time
> "one more minute"
> "time"

4. Confidentiality

Chapter *14*

Conflict

WORKING WITH CONFLICT is one of the greatest challenges we face in our personal lives, as well as in our communities, national politics, and international relations. In this chapter, I will focus on interpersonal conflict, but the principles presented here would go a long way in easing broader conflicts within and among nations.

In situations of conflict, we are especially challenged to listen and to speak from an inner place of balance and empathy. Conflict triggers the sympathetic nervous system, generating fight-or-flight reflexes that can quickly override the wisdom and compassion of the sovereign self. Even if we have enough self-mastery to resist the primal urge to lash out physically or to flee, we are in a state of emotional arousal—frustrated, angry, confused—that demands relief. The chances of doing or saying something we will later regret are heightened.

The good news is that working with inner conflicts, which has been the focus of much of the practice you have done up to now, is excellent training for working with external ones. Knowing how to be with our own "partial selves" when they are not getting along provides a template for how to be present with others in situations of conflict. Although we can never directly experience someone else's felt sense, we can use our imagination and empathy to put ourselves in their shoes and invite a vicarious felt sense of how things are for them.

Of course, when we are actively in conflict is exactly the hardest time to put ourselves in another person's place. The key to success, just as with intrapersonal conflicts, is being able to separate the two (or more) sides. The first step is to recognize and then get some distance from your own position in the conflict. This takes both self-awareness and self-compassion: "Yes, I notice myself becoming upset about this situation—let me sense how it feels in my body just now." As you connect with the distressing feel of it, give yourself a moment of self-empathy: "Yes, I'm upset; this is painful, hard, unpleasant. I recognize the place in me that is in distress. I am letting it know that it won't get ignored; I will come back to it."

Bringing awareness to the inner, bodily sensations of distress allows you to gain empathic distance from your immediate thoughts and emotions. You can disidentify from your own fixed position and, instead of being driven by it, center yourself in the grounded aware presence of the sovereign self. This gives you the mental and psychological room to consider the matter from the other's point of view. By imagining what's at stake for them, what needs and desires underlie their stated position, you begin to form a vicarious felt sense of where they are coming from: "Oh, that's how this feels for them; this is how they see the situation." Once you have a felt sense for both sides of the conflict, you can also ask yourself, "Is there some way that both our underlying needs can get met?" You are not subordinating or suppressing your own needs but calling on the strength, wisdom, and caring of your sovereign self to honor and include the other person's needs and feelings. This is hard to do, but doubly rewarding when successful.

In the next exercise, you will practice finding your felt sense of a conflict situation and then consciously shifting your attention to developing a vicarious felt sense of the other person's experience. Then we will look at some ways of applying these skills in real time.

Exercise 14.1   Vicarious Felt Sense

Begin by coming into grounded aware presence. When you feel ready, direct your attention to noticing any felt senses, concerns, or situations your body is holding. Give them friendly recognition, but don't go into them. Set them aside, or just let them be, as you rest in a space of simple mindful awareness without goal. When it feels right, bring to mind a particular conflict in your life. If there isn't one that is currently alive for you, think of one from the past—perhaps a situation you wish you could have handled better.

Start telling yourself the story line of the conflict. Do this only as long as it takes to feel emotionally aroused. Then, drop the story line and sense for the feeling beneath the feeling—the felt sense. Give the felt sense some friendly attending, just enough for it to feel clearly recognized. Then let it know you will come back to it later on.

Now, shift your attention to the other person's side of the story, and imagine it as best you are able. Of course, you can't know all of what actually goes on in them, but if you are able to adopt an empathic attitude and imagine the situation from their vantage point, you may after a while evoke a vicarious felt sense of their experience of the conflict. Whatever comes, give it friendly attending. Be with it, without judgment or discursive thought, welcoming it however it is.

If the vicarious felt sense remains vague or elusive, try bringing it into clearer focus by describing and resonating its qualities with words, images, or gestures. When a felt sense of the other person's experience is present for you, move on to empathic inquiry. For example, you can ask, "What is the worst of all this for them?" or "What is at stake for them?" Then ask, "What are they wanting or needing in this situation?"

You can also frame the inquiry as a direct exchange, either with the vicarious felt sense or with the other person (held in your imagination with friendly attending): "What are you wanting or needing?" Or you can imagine yourself in their shoes and ask, "What am I wanting or needing?" Because the felt sense implies limitless possibilities, you may get quite different answers from framing the question in the third person ("What are they wanting?"), second person ("What are you wanting?"), or first person ("What am I wanting?"). Any or all of these can bring fresh insights.

During this process, if you find yourself reacting emotionally from your side of the conflict, take time to acknowledge and bring self-empathy to any feelings of hurt, anger, or confusion. Then recenter yourself in grounded aware presence and try to return to friendly attending to the situation from the other's point of view.

End your session by coming back to your felt sense of the conflict from your own point of view, noticing if it has changed as a consequence of exploring the situation from the other person's perspective. See if you can now find a deeper understanding of the sources of your own feelings. Inquire into what your felt sense is now needing or wanting to have happen. Invite possible action steps for resolving the situation that can be checked against your felt sense for rightness.

One next step in resolving the conflict would be to check the insights from your vicarious felt sense directly with the other person. Do this only if you feel confident you can sustain an attitude of empathic inquiry and not become either aggressive or defensive. You can begin the inquiry by saying something like, "I'm sorry we're not seeing eye to eye. I'd really like to better understand your perspective on this. Would you be willing to share some of the thoughts and feelings behind what you've expressed up to now?" If that open-ended invitation isn't enough, you can try to prompt a response by tentatively sharing your vicarious intuitions: "When you said [or did] _____, I'm wondering if you were feeling [or wanting, needing, looking for, feeling uneasy about, concerned that] _____." Again, try this only if you can do it from a place of sincerity and gentleness in yourself, ready to listen to whatever comes back without getting triggered into attacking or defending. By speaking from your sovereign self rather than your wounded or angry self, you invite the other person to do the same.

Dealing with Conflict in Real Time

Terence, a second-century B.C.E. African slave who became a major Roman playwright, wrote, "Nothing human is alien to me." Even in the midst of conflict, if we can get some distance from the immediacy of our own needs and emotions, then our innate human capacity for empathy and our imaginative capacity to put ourselves in the place of another person can generate real insight into others' experience of the world.

Through empathy and putting ourselves in the other's place, we can even recognize ways in which we ourselves provoked or irritated the other person. Here it is important to maintain self-empathy and not collapse into self-blaming or other feelings of inadequacy. Even as we perceive what in our own behavior was problematic for others, we can still recognize and honor the authentic needs that motivated us. Sometimes an apology will feel right, but be careful about making apologies when you don't really mean them (these usually follow the pattern "I'm sorry . . . *but* . . .").

Although arriving at a shared understanding and resolution of conflict is ideal, it isn't necessary to have perfect agreement or even to resolve all aspects of the situation in order to reach emotional closure. A residue of sadness may remain, accepting that things are not as you wished them to be, but that sadness can coexist with a sense of being at peace. This kind of "positive sadness" often accompanies acceptance; indeed, it is the sign of a genuine acceptance that liberates us to move on with our lives.

Dealing with conflict in real time has the advantage that you don't need to imagine how things are for the other person: they're right there to tell you. The disadvantage, of course, is that you are likely to become triggered into uncomfortable emotions and body states that will block your ability to operate from your best self. One way of mitigating the likelihood of becoming triggered, and of triggering the other person, is simply to agree to take turns speaking. This is especially effective when there is an underlying foundation of mutual respect, friendship, and/or affection.

Exercise 14.2 Taking Turns

Invite the other person to let you know what they are feeling about the situation. Tell them to take as much time as they need, including pauses for thought, and assure them that you will not interrupt or respond until they've expressed everything that's on their mind. You are making a commitment to just listen, even when you are in disagreement and regardless of what emotional reactions get aroused in you. Ask them to let you know when they feel they've said everything they need to for one turn, letting them know they'll get another.

Then request them to listen without saying anything while you take a turn sharing your perspectives, feelings, and needs. Let them know that you may be silent at times to check inside yourself and that you will let them know when you feel complete. Then it will be their turn to share anything that has arisen for them while you were speaking. You can go back and forth like this any number of times, or agree in advance on a certain number of turns or a specific time to end.

There are several things you can do that will contribute greatly to the success of taking turns. First and foremost is to practice friendly attending while the other person is sharing their side of the story. Be genuinely present for them; appreciate them as a unique human being separate from yourself. Take in their words fully as well as their body language, breathing, gestures, and facial expressions. Try to sense the inner source of their words and feelings.

Second, at the beginning of your own turn, *reflect back* what you have heard and understood from the other person, for example: "I hear that you felt ignored and upset when I went ahead without consulting you." Also acknowledge the other person's needs in the situation as they become clear to you: "I hear now that it was really important to you to be consulted first." Identify aspects of the situation where you are in agreement: "I agree that you are a key player in this process." Point to elements of the situation that were affecting both of you: "I know we were both under a lot of pressure to meet the deadline." Where possible, acknowledge what you might have done differently: "I now see clearly that I should have reached out to you before proceeding, and I apologize for not having done so."

Seek first to understand, then to be understood. Once you have sincerely sought to understand the other person through empathic listening, reflection, and acknowledging needs and areas of agreement, you are ready to let the other person know in turn how the situation is for you. Keep coming back to your actual felt sense, using the one-at-a-time structure of the exercise to give yourself as much time as it takes for the right thing to say next to emerge organically. Being real takes time! Stay in touch with your felt sense as you speak, and guard against statements or tones of voice that imply blaming or defensiveness. Gentle sincerity invites empathic listening and understanding from the other: "What was going on for me was that I was on my way into a two-hour meeting and I felt obligated to get back to Paul about this right away."

Identify your underlying needs,* being careful not to confuse your need with taking a fixed *position.* "I need to have a private office" is a position, not a need (even though the word *need* is employed). "My need is for a quiet work space in which I can think and write" states the underlying need. If you have a specific solution in mind, frame it as a request rather than an assertion or a demand: "What would you think of my moving into the empty office on the second floor?"

Even when it is not possible to slow down a conflict by agreeing to take turns, you can still do many of the things described above to moderate the tempo and allow tension to dissipate rather than escalate. The key—and this is where the Mindful Focusing approach differs from conventional conflict resolution methods—is pausing again and again to track your inner felt sense as the exchange unfolds. This allows you to get some space from your own emotional reactions and impulses and at the same time gives the other person space to feel heard, even when their perceptions and feelings are different from your own.

Reflecting can also do a lot to damp down the intensity of an exchange. When skillfully done, reflecting or paraphrasing what the speaker is saying gives them the sensation that they are "getting through," actually being heard, and this has a physiologically

---

*This chapter is indebted to Nonviolent Communication (NVC), a simple but powerful four-step approach to addressing conflict without inflaming emotions. The four steps (developed by Marshall Rosenberg, another student of Carl Rogers) are observations, feelings, needs, and requests. NVC and Focusing skills are highly complementary. For more information, see www.cnvc.org and nvctraining.com.

calming effect. It also gives them the opportunity to correct or amplify prior statements, often gaining more clarity for themselves in the process. Likewise, the other moves described above can all be constructive during a difficult interchange. Here they are in outline form:

- Clear your inner space (GAP)
- Feel empathy for yourself and the other person (friendly attending)
- Listen deeply, staying in touch with your felt sense
- Reflect the other's words and feelings
- Affirm the other's needs
- Affirm areas of mutual agreement
- Acknowledge mistakes and things you could have done differently
- Use empathic inquiry to clarify and deepen understanding on both sides
- Share your feelings and needs (not fixed positions)
- Make requests rather than demands

Approaching conflict in the way I've described is not easy. It takes practice and inevitably involves getting it wrong some of the time. But if we can clear a space in ourselves and disidentify from our own emotional reactions, without suppressing or rejecting them, then our sovereign self can stay centered and respond to whatever arises in the moment, just as a skilled rider responds fluidly to a horse's unpredictable movements.

This chapter has emphasized one-on-one interpersonal conflict, but I strongly believe the framework presented here applies equally to large-scale conflict. Listen to the words of Dag Hammarskjold, the great secretary-general of the United Nations, inventor of shuttle diplomacy and the only person ever to receive a posthumous Nobel Peace Prize, following his 1961 death (or assassination, as much evidence suggests) in a plane crash while mediating a cease-fire in the Congo Crisis:

The door to an understanding of the other party, with whom you may have to deal in business, in politics or in the international sphere, is a fuller understanding of yourself, since the other party, of course, is made fundamentally of the same stuff as you yourself.

Thus, no education is complete, in a world basically united, which does not include man himself, and is not inspired by a recognition of the fact that you will not understand your enemy without understanding yourself, and that an understanding of your enemy will throw considerable light also on yourself and on your own motives.[1]

Chapter 15

Making Tough Decisions

TOUGH DECISIONS involve aspects of all three of the topics treated in the preceding chapters: action steps, relationships, and conflict. We need to do something in the world; what we do affects others; and there's more than one side to the situation. If you spend Thanksgiving with your in-laws in California, you can't be with your parents in New York. If you take the big vacation you've been dreaming about, you can't buy that new car you've been saving up for. In our daily lives, of course, we make small decisions all the time—what to eat, whether to watch TV or go online or read a book, who to call to fix the washing machine. Many of these decisions need no more than a moment's thought; others require research and analysis but are fairly straightforward once we've done our homework. Then there are the tough decisions, the kind where the stakes are high and the best course of action is not easy to discern. These are the kinds of decisions that challenge us to discover what is most important to us, what our real priorities are—ultimately, what our deepest values are.

Living life forward means making decisions in specific situations that also nurture our fundamental well-being and growth by carrying forward our life as a whole. At any moment, many different actions and occurrences might serve to move our life forward, while many others would not. No single course of action can realize all of life's implicit possibilities; some will be realized while others continue to be implicit. This is simply the nature of life, even when lived to the fullest. Our challenge, then, is to find the *most right* direction at any given juncture.

In making tough decisions, finding the most right direction isn't simply a question of choosing among given alternatives. Even though you decide to have Thanksgiving with the in-laws rather than at your parents', the rightness of that choice—whether or not it actually carries your life forward—hangs on the depth and clarity of the inner dialogue between felt sense and reason by which you arrive at the decision. If you spend the holiday feeling resentment and regret, none of your needs are getting met. In the worst case, the pressure of a stopped process is building up more and more, with life-constricting and potentially destructive consequences down the road. On the other hand, if you have consciously identified the importance to your spouse and your spouse's family, therefore to your marriage, therefore to *you*, of making this choice—and have identified and honored your own needs that won't get met this time around but could in the future—then the time spent with your in-laws will move your life forward at a deep level. You can't be in California and New York simultaneously, but you *can* transcend the inner conflict.

Recently my friend Don was torn between joining some new acquaintances for a ski trip in Colorado and accompanying his wife on a work trip to Washington, D.C., that would allow him to spend time with an old college roommate he was still close to. Both were things he really wanted to do, and deciding between them was agonizing. As he contemplated the two competing options, underlying needs, wants, beliefs, and fears came into clearer focus. The ski trip was about his delight in making interesting new acquaintances, the joy of being in the high mountains, the physical thrill of skiing, and an overall feeling of novelty and adventure. Going deeper, he also discovered that the ski trip touched on some anxieties. Perhaps his new friends were super skiers and it would be too challenging to keep up with them. He'd been having some trouble with his back lately. If he got in over his head, he feared, he might lose stature with his new friends and weaken rather than strengthen their friendship.

It is important to recognize that whether Don's fears about his skiing proficiency and losing stature were accurate is less important than the fact that they showed up as he spent time with his felt sense of the situation. Accurate or not, these fears lived in his body at some deep level. All of us have places of fear, shame, anger, and guilt, often shaped by childhood and experiences later in life, but also because this is just the way we're wired to begin with. Touching into such negative feelings can be uncomfortable, but recognizing and befriending them is a royal road to self-knowledge, wise decisions, and energy to live our lives forward.

Overcoming our fears doesn't mean eliminating fear itself. Fear exists to protect our well-being and guide our actions. It is a biological messenger carrying valuable intelligence. To benefit from that intelligence, we need to be brave enough to let the fear show up and deliver its message. If we panic at the mere appearance of fear, we act impulsively and often unwisely. If we try to suppress the fear, we are locking up the messenger before it is able to deliver the message. Only when we are able to feel and befriend the rawness of our fear in the moment can we begin to discern the intelligence in its message.

Because fear and other negative emotions are inheritances from millennia of animal evolution as well as human socialization, the message can to a greater or lesser degree be out of date. It may not need to be taken literally. But we have to begin by hearing it literally in order to discern how it applies in the present. This often calls for empathic inquiry, in effect a dialogue between the emotion and the sovereign self in which old and perhaps outdated aspects of the fear can be brought to light and updated. What comes at first as "I won't be able to keep up" or "I'll lose stature" becomes "Something in me is concerned for my safety and well-being." Figuring out what is really at stake can illuminate which parts of the message are out of date—after all, this messenger began its journey in the distant past—and what about it is up to date and applicable in the present.

As Don spent more time with this seemingly simple choice between two appealing options, a deeper insight came to him. The fears about not being able to keep up and losing stature were there, but beneath them was something much larger. Don was in his sixties, still working but between jobs at the moment, searching for a new position in his field with similar status and compensation as his previous ones but less pressure. He wasn't ready to retire, but he was wanting to slow down a bit. The ski trip was about more than skiing and new friends and having a great time. It was also about aging, losing physical strength and agility, the approach of a time when the passions of his youth might be beyond his reach.

The Washington trip, on the other hand, was about long-term relationships, quiet meals, sharing memories and stories and feelings—all the things that older people enjoy. Don saw the irony: the youthful-feeling ski trip represented his past, whereas the old-feeling Washington trip represented his present and future. Not without some pain and sadness, Don decided on Washington. He wasn't ready to let go of skiing yet—a couple of months later, he took his daughter for a fabulous spring ski trip at a new mountain in Utah—but something had started to change for him. He had let go of a priority that he was beginning to see as belonging more to his past, and affirmed the deeper value of family and friendship in his present and future. His life was living itself forward.

Separating the Sides

When we have a problem or face a difficult decision, we are deal-ing with two or more needs, wants, or goals that are in conflict. By clearly recognizing the different sides that are in tension, we can separate them like fighting children and give our full atten-tion to the felt sense underlying each. By uncovering the deeper need or want that motivates each side of the conflict, we prepare the ground for a solution that honors the needs, interests, and feelings that seemed so opposed to each other.

Honoring a need is not the same as meeting it. The "most right" course of action tries to satisfy the most important needs in a given situation. But decisions involve choices: other needs judged less important may go unmet. Recognizing and acknowl-edging all of the needs and interests that are present—both our own and other people's—honors their validity.

Good decisions are decisions that come from your sovereign self. Having listened to all sides and considered all relevant fac-tors, like a wise parent, elder, or friend, the sovereign self stands back and allows the best decision to emerge organically from the felt sense. It acknowledges each need as valid in its own way but weighs all of them against a felt sense of the situation as a whole.

The sovereign self, while it is unbiased, is not devoid of feel-ing. It feels the rightness of a good decision and is energized by it; at the same time, it may feel sadness, even some pain, about the needs that are not getting met. Don's sadness at giving up the Colorado trip is an example. This kind of positive sadness is a natural component of wise decision making.

Tough decisions in work and organizational contexts are not fundamentally different. The reasoning that goes into such a de-cision will involve different factors; there may be more interests in tension—the needs and rights of individuals versus what's best for the organization, financial constraints, short-term versus long-term objectives, impacts on morale, and so on—but coming to the most right decision, the course of action that best moves the *whole* situation forward, still requires the insight and affirmation that come only from the felt sense.

Some of the harder decisions, for example, that leaders and managers have to make involve letting employees go. Rarely are these situations black and white; there are almost always aspects of the person's work and the person himself or herself that are positive and praiseworthy. Unfortunately, legalities and the need to protect the rest of the organization often make it difficult for a supervisor to fully acknowledge these positive aspects, either to the employee or to other staff. Tough decisions are tough because they're hard to make and, in leadership roles, they affect other people's lives. Especially when one can't publicly share all the tangible and intangible factors that have gone into a tough decision, coming to clarity and conviction in one's felt sense is a key to being able to move ahead wholeheartedly.

What Is Ready to Die Here?

The toughest decisions compel us to achieve clarity about our own deepest values. They can challenge our very sense of who we are. We are called upon not just to do the right thing out in the world but to grow and change in our depths. Just as the cells that make up our living body are continually dying and being born, aspects of our psychological makeup may also need to die when they no longer serve a positive function in our lives. The question "What is ready to die here?" may seem harsh, but it opens the gate to the intimately related question "What is ready to be born?"

Sometimes this dying and birthing process happens on its own, perhaps imperceptibly over time; more often, it takes work. We need to first recognize that there is something in us—a habitual pattern, a strongly held belief or opinion, an attitude about ourselves or others—that no longer fits. Having recognized it, we have to let go of this aspect of ourselves, let it die. Because it may have served us well up to now, or just because it has been a member of our internal family, this is likely to bring sadness. Sometimes there is also regret—we have seen something about ourselves we were blind to. There is a bittersweetness in these moments of realization, a positive sadness that is tender toward the past and open to the future.

Exercise 15.1   Deciding from the Felt Sense

Settle your body and bring awareness inside. When you feel grounded, clear, and present, bring to mind a decision you are facing—for yourself personally, in a relationship or family matter, at work, for a group you're part of, or in a creative process. Using the felt-sense decision protocol below, contemplate all the inner parts as well as external factors, interests, and stakeholders involved in the decision.

Not all of the steps or specific questions in the protocol may apply to every decision. Use the ones that do apply, and feel free to form new questions that better fit your issue. You may need to work your way through the protocol more than once before you reach a decision that feels wholly right and complete in your felt sense.

Felt-Sense Decision Protocol

1. Gather and understand relevant information.
   - external facts and factors that may limit or broaden my options
   - feelings, views, and interests of other people involved in or affected by the decision
2. Separate and listen to the sides.
   - Let each side or part or point of view emerge fully and clearly. If there are other parties involved, consider their interests and try to get a vicarious felt sense of

what's at stake for them. Pause to spend time with felt senses as they arise.

- What is the most important thing for this part or party?
- What is it [what are they] wanting or not wanting?
- Is something for this part or party ready to die or be let go?
- Is something new ready to be born, appear, or manifest?

3. Ask your sovereign self.
   - Like a wise and caring parent who has heard each child's needs and feelings, but knows she must find the best decision for all, center awareness in your sovereign self and evoke a felt sense of the situation as a whole.
     - What is most important in all this? What's truly at stake for me and for all?
     - What am I fearing? What am I wanting?
     - Is something old (in the situation, in myself) ready to die?
     - Is something new ready to be born?

4. Contemplate options.
   - Given all of the above, what feels like the "most right" course of action? Invite novel possibilities, even ones that seem odd or outrageous. What element of truth do they contain?
   - Can the deeper needs of all parts and parties be met? If not, can plans be made for meeting needs in the future that won't be met now?
   - Am I clear and at peace about needs or interests that won't get met by this decision? Acknowledge positive sadness if it arises.

5. Reflect and resonate.
   - How would it feel in my body to do this? Does it fit with my deepest values?

> ➤ Is there still some hidden bias? To check for bias, imagine making a different decision and notice if any unexpected new insight or energy appears.
>
> ➤ Does this decision reflect the attributes of the sovereign self: clarity, confidence, accountability, caring, and skill?

6. Seal your intention.

> ➤ Some decisions can be fully settled in a single session and enacted with a simple action step—making a flight reservation or a telephone call, or speaking up in a meeting. If this is the case, end your session either by taking the required action right away or by inwardly committing yourself to a definite plan for when, where, and how you will accomplish it.
>
> ➤ Many decisions, especially if they involve other people, can't be completed in a single session. As new options surface, further iterations of step one may be needed to gather additional information and views. In these cases, end your session by making sure you are clear on the right next step or steps to move the process forward in a timely way, understanding that new input may call for new rounds of felt-sensing before the matter is fully resolved.

Since felt senses are by definition the discreet experiences of particular individuals, this decision-making protocol emphasizes inner steps to be done on one's own (or, if possible, with the support of a listening partner). It does not take into account the complex dynamics of group process. That said, you can use many of these inner moves even as you are participating in group dialogue, and they can also be adapted for structuring a decision-making process for the whole group.

Chapter 16

Under-Standing

*Do not leave it, do not course over it, as if it were
understood, but instead follow it down until you see
it in the mystery of its own specificity and strength.*

— ANNIE DILLARD[1]

ETYMOLOGISTS ARE unclear about the origins of the English word *understanding*. It has been suggested that the *under-* part of the word comes from the Latin *inter-*, meaning standing among or in the middle of things, that is, close enough to see them clearly. But I prefer to take *under-* literally. When we truly under-stand something, we don't just perceive it; we feel a deeper knowing about its true nature. To do this, we need to get under first appearances and habitual thoughts and reactions. As Annie Dillard says, we need to "follow it down." We need to get a felt sense of the thing.

This deeper, bodily felt kind of understanding is essential to forming and sustaining genuine relationships with other people, as we have been exploring. It is also important in education, professional development, art, literature, philosophy, and religion. Too often we go directly from acquiring information to regurgitating or acting on it. We miss the vital "under" dimension of things. We don't allow them to digest properly and, as a result, we don't absorb things fully and aren't nurtured by them. We don't have them viscerally.

Most of us learned as children not to go swimming right after a meal: even if we aren't consciously aware of it, the body needs its own time for the transformative process of digestion. Understanding works the same way. After we have gathered the data, the input, and perhaps spent some time chewing it over, we need to leave things alone. We need to leave *ourselves* alone so that the invisible digestive processes of understanding can occur. Sometimes the wait is brief—*Aha, I get it*! But often we need to restrain the impulse to rush into speech or action and allow a gap, a clearing, in which something fresh can appear. Think of those Magic Eye pictures.

Works of art, because they draw so much on the felt sense of their makers, are particularly effective for cultivating our ability to understand things in a visceral rather than an intellectual way. Music is perhaps the most direct means for doing this; like the felt sense itself, it can embody immediate felt meaning independent of a story line. Painting and sculpture are also mostly word-free but can be realistic—portraying recognizable people, places, and things—or abstract. Abstract art, in particular, can be understood as the artist's way of conveying felt sense stripped of conventional meanings and associations. Vasily Kandinsky, one of the originators of abstraction in art, began by literally replacing recognizable features in a painting, such as a face, with abstract bits of shape and color.

Writing, and especially poetry, presents a special challenge since it is composed of words, which by definition convey conceptual meanings. Often it is by using words in unconventional ways that a poet points to the underlying felt sense. Emily Dickinson is a brilliant exemplar of this method. Another approach is to eliminate story line and logical argument in favor of just a series of vivid images. T. S. Eliot, in the introduction to his translation of St.-John Perse's long poem "Anabasis," counsels the reader to "allow the images to fall into his memory successively without questioning the reasonableness of each at the moment; so that, at the end, a total effect is produced."[2]

Here is a short but exquisite poem that builds up a series of seemingly unrelated images, each conveyed with extraordinary economy, that virtually require one to respond from the felt sense.

Exercise 16.1   Reading with the Felt Sense

Read the poem several times, silently and aloud, slower and faster, letting the images fall into your memory, as T. S. Eliot advises. Savor it, be intimate with it, "follow it down" into the mystery of its own special resonance. (Later do the same with a poem of your choosing, or a work of art or piece of music.)

Briefly It Enters, and Briefly Speaks

BY JANE KENYON

I am the blossom pressed in a book,
found again after two hundred years. . . .

I am the maker, the lover, and the keeper. . . .

When the young girl who starves
sits down to a table
she will sit beside me. . . .

I am food on the prisoner's plate. . . .

I am water rushing to the wellhead,
filling the pitcher until it spills. . . .

I am the patient gardener
of the dry and weedy garden. . . .

I am the stone step,
the latch, and the working hinge. . . .

I am the heart contracted by joy. . . .
the longest hair, white
before the rest. . . .

I am there in the basket of fruit
presented to the widow. . . .

I am the musk rose opening
unattended, the fern on the boggy summit. . . .

I am the one whose love
overcomes you, already with you
when you think to call my name. . . .[3]

For the sake of brevity and because I love poetry, the exercise given here involves reading a poem. But the theme of this chapter is understanding in general. Learning any new thing, be it history or chemistry or Spanish, a new technology or job responsibility, how to ski or play the cello, involves a similar unconscious digestive body process. Trungpa Rinpoche called this interval "the yogurt phase."

When I was a freshman at Harvard, I had the great fortune to take what we called Hum 6 (Humanities 6), a famous general education course taught by the renowned English professor and critic Reuben Brower. Professor Brower advocated what he called "reading in slow motion"—a careful and very personal close reading of literary texts. His first questions were: "What is it like to read this poem? With what feeling are we left at its close?" Only from our personal response to those questions would he allow students to engage in "critical thinking" and interpretation of the works we were studying. There's an essential point here. Understanding through the felt sense is not in opposition to conceptual thinking. Rather, it is the very foundation for original, meaningful thought.

Chapter 17

"First Thought Best Thought": The Felt Sense in Creative Process

Isadora Duncan, founder of modern dance, wrote about her youthful explorations of movement:

> For hours I would stand quite still, my two hands folded between my breasts, covering the solar plexus. My mother often became alarmed to see me remain for such long intervals quite motionless as if in a trance—but I was seeking and I finally discovered the central spring of all movements, the crater of motor power, the unity from which all diversities of movements are born.[1]

What Duncan called "the central spring," Chögyam Trungpa (a prolific artist in his own right) called "first thought." Trungpa once cowrote a poem with Allen Ginsberg, the iconic Beat poet who was also his devoted student, in which Trungpa gave as the opening line, "First thought is best, then you compose." Ginsberg later reduced this to the phrase "first thought best thought." This slogan has gained some notoriety but is often misunderstood to mean "Be spontaneous, just go with the first thing that pops into your head." As Trungpa himself later clarified, that was not his real meaning. What he was pointing to was precisely the need to be in touch with the preconceptual, preform source or seed—he also referred to it as "first dot"—from which authentic artistic expression arises. Far from being the first random idea that comes to mind, "first thought" means touching into a more primal level of experience than conventional thought altogether. As his original line had it, first thought is best, *then* you compose.

For Trungpa, with his deep contemplative training as well as innate creative gift, the gap between first thought and composition tended to be brief. His process of creating a poem or calligraphy or flower arrangement appeared to be spontaneous and without second thoughts. Yet an attentive observer could feel the power of his inner centeredness, the way his words or gestures arose from a deep, nonconceptual source. Isadora Duncan, on the other hand, describes standing still for hours to find her "crater of motor power." Most of us ordinary mortals will be situated somewhere between those two poles in the tempo of our creative process.

One doesn't have to be a trained artist to let the creative juices flow. Cooking, gardening, rearranging a room, and many other everyday activities lend themselves to dipping into the felt sense. Trungpa was a great advocate of what he called "art in everyday life," which he explained as "an appreciation of things as they are and of what one is—which produces an enormous spark. Something happens—clicks—and the poet writes poems, the painter paints pictures, the musician composes music."

My own inner artist loves creating little haiku poems. Here's one I just wrote:

> Birds chirping outdoors,
> phone chirping in the next room—
> getting down to work.

Although I don't adhere to most of the aesthetic principles and compositional rules of the venerable Japanese haiku tradition, I do stick strictly to the traditional format of three lines consisting of five, seven, and five syllables each. I find I need the structure, the constraint, provided by this form to challenge me deeper into my felt sense. Often, if I start out with lines that have too many or too few syllables, the requirements of the form direct me back to the nonverbal, felt source of those lines. New lines that meet the syllable requirements won't mean exactly the same thing as the original ones, but they must articulate the original felt sense. I am made to ask inside, what am I *really* feeling? Just as in the focusing step of resonating quality words, images, or gestures against an unclear felt sense, the feeling or insight I began with crystallizes more precisely through this process.

By way of illustration, the last line of my haiku, "getting down to work," took some time to show up. There's a leap involved — noticing bird chirps could lead to an infinite variety of next thoughts, feelings, or memories. This morning it led me to notice scratchy sounds issuing from the next room, my wife's conference call for her work, audible but not clear enough for me to make out actual words. Having already registered the birds' chirping from outdoors, I recognized these indistinct speaker-phone sounds as also being chirps. Hence the second line.

The new associations of indoors versus outdoors, other people at work, and unclear meanings moves the poem in a certain direction, both narrowing its scope and opening it to new possibilities. Now there is a tension, something unresolved: two things that are mostly different have something in common, but so what? How does this relate to the bigger picture? At first I felt only that tension — birds chirping / telephone chirping. It was pleasing to have found this connection, but it wants more. What's at stake here for me? What's the deeper source of this clever comparison? After a pregnant pause came a sudden insight, accompanied by a felt shift in my body: this is actually about the challenge for me of getting to work. It is the effort to focus attention on my intended purpose — the next chapter of my book — that has caused me to notice other things in the environment, things I'll need to *not* attend to in order to undertake the inner process of writing. With this, the five-syllable line "getting down to work" emerged at once, resolving the felt tension and completing the poem with an unexpected twist.

One of the things I love about the haiku form is how it implies everything I've just rather laboriously spelled out, and much more, but the reader has to find his or her own way of making sense of the highly compressed language. That third line in particular is, at first blush, a non sequitur. Are the birds getting down to work? In a way, yes. Are the people on the conference call getting down to work? Definitely. But the unexpected twist, the flash of fresh insight, is that this is really about *me* getting down to work.

My little haiku is not immortal poetry, but I hope it indicates to some degree the role of the felt sense in creative process—the need for going to the nonconceptual source, and the novel understanding and expression that can emerge there. I also want to say that creative expression, even when it is not on a high level of accomplishment, is valuable to the creator to the extent that they have found something fresh in their own experience, something that carries their life process forward, if only in a small, subtle way.

Following my morning work session, I went for a walk with Luna. These walks are frequently the occasion for a new haiku—not because I have the intention to "write a haiku" but because something in the environment strikes me as unusual, vivid, or moving. This afternoon, it was the few remaining patches of snow, remnants of a series of unusually heavy late winter snowfalls that extended right into the first week of spring.

Last patches of snow,
grimed with gravel and dead leaves,
yield to crocuses.

On the one hand, this is a quite ordinary observation—anyone out today would have noticed the shrinking piles of snow and especially the yellow and purple crocuses just emerging through the detritus of winter. But it also expresses a very particular moment of experience and feeling, something triggered by seeing the melting snow, dirty and diminished, a pathetic remnant of February's record-breaking blizzard that buried us in more than two feet of wind-drifted snow and caused the governor to ban car traffic for twenty-four hours. Pathetic yet somehow endearing.

When I had just the dirty snow piles and the crocuses, I came up with a nice five-syllable third line: "yellow and purple." Those fresh, vivid colors contrasting with the dirty white snow and the general brownness of early spring pleasingly evoked the transition from old burdens to new life. But when I checked against my felt experience, I saw that this was too much attention on the crocuses and not enough on the main trigger of my feeling, those dirty, rather pathetic snow piles. It took several tries to come up with "grimed with gravel and dead leaves," but I found it by staying with my felt sense of what had moved me in the first place and checking possible descriptions against it. And by some alchemy that we don't really understand, the felt sense generated the gritty and gratifyingly alliterative phrase "grimed with gravel," a perfect marriage of sound and sense. Likewise, it took a few tries to come up with the wonderful word *yields*, which seems to capture both the diminishment of the snow and the curiously endearing quality I felt in it. Finally, the odd-sounding word *crocuses* gives just the right touch of spring. The word itself introduces fresh color; it doesn't need purple and yellow to make its point.

Forgive me for imposing my amateur poetic efforts on you. My intention is simply to stimulate your own seeds of creativity, which I invite you to engage now.

Exercise 17.1 Composing a Haiku

Experiment for yourself with the three-line haiku form. Don't worry about counting syllables to begin with, but keep in mind the basic progression:

1. Initial observation
2. Elaborating or qualifying the observation
3. A leap or twist, fresh perception or insight, more-than-logical, sparked from the felt sense

The three lines don't have to come to you in order. Sometimes the leap—the fresh perception or thought—may come first. Then the challenge is to consult your felt sense to find the source or background of that novel perception.

When you have three lines that seem to capture your experience, see if you can modify them to meet the 5-7-5 syllable count. The key is to check the new lines against your felt sense. They should preserve the essence of the original inspiration and deepen or sharpen it in ways that feel even more right.

To inspire you, here are two further examples, the first from Matsuo Basho (in Sam Hamill's translation) and a second from Chögyam Trungpa. Basho's haiku adheres to the seventeen-syllable form, whereas Trungpa's is freer in form, but both illustrate the three-line observation/expansion/leap progression.

> Azaleas placed
> carefully—and a woman
> shredding dried codfish.

> Skiing in a red and blue outfit,
> Drinking cold beer with a lovely smile—
> I wonder if I'm one of them.

Chapter *18*

Enlarging Space

IN MUCH OF WHAT has been presented so far, the importance of feeling warmth has been emphasized—being heartfelt, gentle, and caring. The sovereign self is enlivened by warmth. At the same time, it possesses a cool aspect. This is the coolness of dispassion, of seeing things as they are, free from our own hopes and fears. Chögyam Trungpa used to describe mindfulness meditation as "cool boredom." This may sound unappealing, but the experience he was pointing to is an essential aspect of wisdom. It is cool like a brilliant winter day, when every detail of the environment stands out clearly: cold but spacious, unentertaining yet vividly present.

Here is a poem by Wallace Stevens that powerfully evokes the ultimate of cool boredom:

The Snow Man

One must have a mind of winter
To regard the frost and the boughs
Of the pine-trees crusted with snow;

And have been cold a long time
To behold the junipers shagged with ice,
The spruces rough in the distant glitter

Of the January sun; and not to think
Of any misery in the sound of the wind,
In the sound of a few leaves,

Which is the sound of the land
Full of the same wind
That is blowing in the same bare place

For the listener, who listens in the snow,
And, nothing himself, beholds
Nothing that is not there and the nothing that is.[1]

This poem is often interpreted as nihilistic, evoking the emptiness of a world devoid of human emotion and meaning making.
But I believe it is ultimately positive. The snowman/observer
who is "nothing himself" is not a meaningless void but rather an
unbiased, dispassionate knower who does not project his own desires and fears onto the world. He sees "nothing that is not there."
He also sees "the nothing that is"—the infinite intricacy of things
just as they are.

Beholding the vast space and vivid detail of the natural
world—not only in winter but at any season of the year—can en-
large our inner felt space. Just as the earth and sky accommodate
an endless array of features and creatures, the sovereign self is a
space of greater awareness that accommodates the intricacy and
variegated textures of all our perceptions, thoughts, and feelings.

Here is a version of the very first exercise presented in this
book, Grounded Aware Presence, expanded to encompass the
world of nature and our human presence in it.

Exercise 18.1   Enlarging Space

Go outdoors to a garden, park, or natural area. Find a quiet
spot that affords a view of plants, trees, earth, rocks, and so
forth, as well as a view toward the distant skyline (whether

natural or constructed). If possible, sit down directly on the earth, or on a convenient stone or log. Settle your body and feel its weight sink down into the support of the earth. After a while, say softly to yourself, "Grounded on the earth."

Concentrating awareness in your sense of sight, focus on a plant, stone, or other natural object no more than five feet away from you. Look at it as if you have never seen anything like it before. Perceive it freshly, vividly, appreciating its unique qualities of shape, color, texture, movement. Take in its presence, here and now. Let go of discursive thoughts that arise.

Then refocus your gaze on something a bit farther off, perhaps 15 to 30 feet away. Again, see it as if for the very first time. Let its unique features become vividly present for you. If possible, do the same with a natural object in the middle distance, 50 to 150 feet from you.

Then pick a spot on the horizon or skyline and gaze at it, letting go of any thoughts that arise, staying with the visual details and feeling the simple presence of whatever your eyes are resting on.

Finally, let your gaze go out to the sky itself. Perhaps there are clouds or mist, perhaps just endless blue. Sense the sky's depth and vastness. Without changing the focus of your gaze, become aware of your entire field of vision, everything visible out to the periphery of what you can see. Now bring in the other sense perceptions—sounds of birds or leaves or water, smells of earth or grass or flowers, the touch of the wind on your skin, the rough earth against your body.

Sense the unified totality of everything you are aware of just now. Say softly, "Aware of all of it."

Sustain this open awareness for as long as you can, dropping any discursive thinking and resisting the temptation to redirect your gaze to an object on the periphery. Imagine you have just arrived from Mars and nothing you see is familiar.

Everything is abstract color, form, and texture, but extraordinarily vivid.

You are also aware of being aware. Bringing a hand to your heart, feel your own presence. Gradually extend your sense of being present in your body to include the whole of space. You are present in the wide world, part of it, here and now. Say softly, "Present in this world."

Let the outer and inner spaces coexist in your awareness. You may even have glimpses of nondual awareness, an experience in which the felt difference between outside and inside, self and other, dissolves.

If time and space permit, you can go directly into the next exercise. Or save it for another time.

Exercise 18.2 Wandering with Wonder

Go into nature. Find a quiet spot and stand still there. Keeping your eyes open, go through the steps of Grounded Aware Presence. For Grounded, bring attention to the contact of your feet with the ground and let your weight sink down into the earth's support. For Aware, center attention in sight as well as hearing. For Present, bring your hand to your heart and feel present both in your body and in the larger space around you.

Let your attention be drawn to a flower, leaf, branch, stone, or other natural object. See it as if for the first time. Contemplate it, taking in all of its features and qualities. Let it become vividly present to you.

Without losing sight of the outer object, bring awareness inside and notice if there is a corresponding felt sense. There may be little there at first, but wait patiently with friendly attending (both to the object and to your inner awareness) and see if a felt sense forms after a while. Note any thoughts that arise, and keep returning attention to your double awareness of the object and your felt sense. Let the felt sense deepen, change, or shift in any way it wants to.

Wander aimlessly, allowing different objects to catch your attention, spending time with each in turn. Contemplate each object and gradually sense what comes for you in a bodily felt way. As you leave each object of contemplation, appreciate its presence in the world. Say, or feel, a silent thank-you. Between objects, walk slowly, feel the earth beneath your feet, and open all your senses—hearing, smell, and touch as well as sight. Feel your motion through the world.

I'll close this chapter with a wonderful quotation from Johann Wolfgang von Goethe, the great German romantic poet who was also a pioneering scientist:

The human being knows himself only insofar as he knows the world; he perceives the world only in himself, and himself only in the world. Every new object, clearly seen, opens up a new organ of perception in us.[2]

Chapter 19

Contemplation: Sensing for the More

THE ORIENTATION of this book has been toward you as an individual, finding and cultivating your inner felt sense, growing the capacity of your sovereign self, and carrying forward the intricate and beautiful life process embodied in your unique existence. In concluding, I would like to point briefly toward a kind of carrying forward that is larger than any one individual's life story and personal experiences.

This larger context has two dimensions. There is the "more than me" dimension—other people, the communities we are part of, other communities and cultures and species, people who lived in times past and struggled and survived to create and sustain human society for us to inherit, people yet to be born who we hope will sustain and build on our legacy. There is also the "more than I" dimension—some greater space or consciousness or power that transcends our sense of self altogether. It is the realm of the spiritual, of transformation, of the self becoming, or dissolving into, more than itself. Zen master Dogen encapsulates both the "more than me" and the "more than I" in a beautiful and profoundly paradoxical description of the path of spiritual awakening:

> To study the buddha way is to study the self. To study the self is to forget the self. To forget the self is to be actualized by myriad things.[1]

For me, the essence of the spiritual is not some end state of enlightenment or salvation but rather this always present possibility of becoming "more." It is a paradoxical kind of becoming more because it is also a becoming less, a letting-go of our old sense of self. Like the snake shedding its skin or the butterfly emerging from its chrysalis, we can break free from that which has contained and protected and identified us up to now, and emerge fresh, vulnerable, perhaps fearful, but ready for a new stage of our journey.

In chapter 15, we saw that making tough decisions often involves asking challenging questions: What's at stake here for me? What is ready to die? What is ready to be born? When we apply these kinds of deep questions to ourselves, they become challenges to self-transcendence: What is at stake for me as a person? What in me or about me is ready to die? What wants to take birth freshly in me? Are situations that seem to have no satisfactory solution challenging me to grow, to change, to become more than I have been—stronger, gentler, more responsible, more loving? Are they inviting me, perhaps, to come alive in a whole new way?

In decision making, we work on solving the situation; in self-transcendence, it is more like the situation is solving us. Having differentiated ourselves as unique individuals, we experience a dissolving or reintegration into something larger. At times self-transcendence happens abruptly, perhaps from the impact of powerful events beyond our control. We can also consciously open ourselves to a more incremental transformation process through contemplative practices such as Mindful Focusing. The core dynamic of contemplative practices is pausing the momentum of everyday activity and thought and holding our attention still long enough to let something emerge, in its own time and its own way, from the infinitely generative realm of our not yet formed knowing. This knowing is implicit in our living body.

Because body processes are slower than mental processes, nothing may come for a long time. What is important is not to be overcome by impatience, doubt, or discouragement but simply to wait and give our felt sense, our body-knowing, as much time as it needs. T. S. Eliot describes this kind of radical waiting in his deeply contemplative *Four Quartets*:

> Wait without thought, for you are not ready for thought:
> So the darkness shall be the light, and the stillness the
> dancing.[2]

Self-transcendence can also feel like returning to the deep source of our being. William Butler Yeats's late poem "A Dialogue of Self and Soul," a passionate confrontation with his own sense of identity, concludes:

> I am content to follow to its source
> Every event in action or in thought;
> Measure the lot; forgive myself the lot!
> When such as I cast out remorse
> So great a sweetness flows into the breast
> We must laugh and we must sing,
> We are blest by everything,
> Everything we look upon is blest.[3]

Those last two lines are a thrilling evocation of the "more than me" dimension—the community of all beings, of all existence, what Buddhist teacher Thich Nhat Hanh calls "interbeing." As we come to recognize our subselves, our own multipleness, we also come to realize that we in turn are subselves of a larger constellation. When deeply felt, this realization is spiritual, but also ethical, cultural, and historical. We participate in a reciprocal dynamic by which social, economic, and environmental stresses drive individuals to deepen their self-understanding and undergo personal transformations that, in turn, power the engines of social and cultural change. The personal is political, and the spiritual is practical. "In our age," said Dag Hammarskjold, "the road to holiness necessarily passes through the world of action."

The following exercise marks an end and also, I hope, a beginning. It invites you to apply the felt-sensing skills you have been developing to the spiritual practice of contemplation. I offer it as a complement to whatever spiritual, religious, philosophical, and ethical resources you already have. It is not meant to replace but to deepen and enrich.

Exercise 19.1   Sensing for the More

Below are seven statements. They might feel true for you, or they might not. Say them silently and/or out loud. Try out the alternate words suggested in parentheses; substitute your own words. Wait; be with your felt sense; notice what comes for you in response to each statement. Something may come as a felt sense or a realization or both together. Whatever comes, stay with it gently, take it in, contemplate it. If nothing comes in relation to one of the statements, or if what comes doesn't feel true or fresh, wait some more before moving on. Nothing has to come; the waiting itself is enough.

- Something in my sense of identity [who I am, what I'm all about] no longer fits [serves me well, feels right . . .].
- Something is ready to die [let go, dissolve, change . . .].
- Something is ready to be born [appear, come alive, manifest . . .].
- To study the self is to forget the self.
- The darkness shall be the light, and the stillness the dancing.

➤ The road to holiness passes through the world of action.
➤ We are blest by everything; everything we look upon is blest.

Wisdom can be found anywhere, everywhere. The sentences above are merely suggestions reflecting some of the themes of this book and others' words of wisdom that I myself have found meaningful. You will find your own sources for contemplation in the context and events of your own life, perhaps from a sacred text, a poem, a song, a movie, a friend's caring words, or your own freshly arriving words or images. Contemplate, sense for the more, trust your felt sense.

And don't be afraid to just wait. Let us end where we began, with John Keats's evocative description of negative capability: "capable of being in uncertainties, Mysteries, doubts, without any irritable reaching after fact & reason."

Appendix: Mindful Focusing Protocol

1. Grounded Aware Presence (GAP)
   - center attention at your base (grounded), head (aware), and heart (presence)
   - (brief version) settle your body, drop thinking, bring awareness inside your torso
2. Finding the felt sense
   - assume an attitude of friendly attending
   - notice what your body is holding—"something" or "something in me" (or)
   - ask, "What wants my attention just now?" (or)
   - start with a situation
     - recollect the situation freshly for a minute or two
     - drop the story line
     - sense for the feeling beneath the feeling
3. Bringing the felt sense into focus
   - describe its felt qualities using a word, phrase, metaphor, image, or gesture
   - resonate—does the description fit? does the felt sense like it?
4. Empathic inquiry
   - pose a question and wait for the felt sense to respond
     - "What makes it [you, me] feel so _____?"
     - "What is the worst part of all this?"
     - "What is it [are you, am I] fearing?"
     - "What is it [are you, am I] wanting?"

5. Appreciating what came
   - notice and receive any small steps, felt shifts, and insights
   - after receiving, ask inside, "Is there more?"
   - choose when to stop for now
     - journal (recommended)
   - thank your body
6. Transitioning back to the world
   - return to a sense of grounded aware presence
   - gently open your awareness outward; notice and freshly appreciate your surroundings
   - sense your own presence within and as part of the larger environment

Notes

Introduction

1. Carl R. Rogers, *On Becoming a Person: A Therapist's View of Psychotherapy* (Boston: Houghton Mifflin, 1961), 17.

Chapter 1: Steps toward Finding the Felt Sense

1. John Keats, *Complete Poems and Selected Letters of John Keats* (New York: Modern Library, 2001), 492.

Chapter 5: Working with Situations

1. Eugene Gendlin, *A Process Model* (Spring Valley, New York: The Focusing Institute, 1997), 233.

Chapter 10: Mindfulness, Awareness, and the Sovereign Self

1. Jon Kabat-Zinn, *Wherever You Go, There You Are* (New York: Hyperion, 1994), 4.
2. Chögyam Trungpa, *Work, Sex, Money: Real Life on the Path of Mindfulness* (Boston: Shambhala Publications, 2011), 208.

Chapter 11: The Deep Nature of Life Process

1. V. S. Ramachandran, quoted in Thomas Metzinger, *The Ego Tunnel: The Science of the Mind and the Myth of the Self* (New York: Basic Books, 2009), 109–10.

Chapter 13: Deep Listening

1. Daniel Siegel, *Mindsight: The New Science of Personal Transformation* (New York: Bantam Books, 2010), 27.
2. Martin Luther King, Jr., *Strength to Love* (Minneapolis, Minn.: Fortress Press, 1981), 119.

Chapter 14: Conflict

1. Dag Hammarskjold, quoted in Roger Lipsey, *Hammarskjold: A Life* (Anne Arbor, Mich.: University of Michigan Press, 2013) 193.

Chapter 16: Under-Standing

1. Annie Dillard, "Write Till You Drop," *New York Times*, May 28, 1989.
2. T. S. Eliot, *Anabasis: St.-John Perse* (New York: Harcourt, Brace, 1938), 10.
3. Jane Kenyon, *Collected Poems* (Saint Paul: Graywolf Press, 2005), 137. Used by permission of Graywolf Press.

Chapter 17: "First Thought Best Thought"

1. Isadora Duncan, quoted in Gendlin, *A Process Model*, 216.

Chapter 18: Enlarging Space

1. Wallace Stevens, *The Collected Poems of Wallace Stevens* (New York: Vintage Books, 1990), 9.
2. Johann Wolfgang von Goethe, *Scientific Studies* (Princeton, N.J.: Princeton University Press, 1988), 39.

Chapter 19: Contemplation

1. Dogen, *Treasury of the True Dharma Eye* (Boston: Shambhala Publications, 2010), 30.
2. Excerpt from *Four Quartets* by T. S. Eliot. Copyright © 1943 by T. S. Eliot and renewed 1971 by Esme Valerie Eliot. Used by permission of Houghton Mifflin Harcourt Publishing Company and Faber and Faber, Inc. All rights reserved.
3. W. B. Yeats, *Collected Poems* (New York: Scribner, 1996), 236.

Resources for Further Study and Practice

Online

www.mindfulfocusing.com. My own web site, on which you will find a schedule of upcoming programs and phone classes, my blog, free articles and recordings, and more. I also offer private coaching/guiding sessions. My e-mail is david@mindfulfocusing .com.

www.focusingresources.org. The web site of Ann Weiser Cornell, originator of Inner Relationship Focusing, and her colleagues. Free articles, audio and other resources, and a rich offering of phone courses, private sessions, and residential intensive programs.

www.focusing.org. The web site of the Focusing Institute, the central organization for Focusing worldwide: writings of Eugene Gendlin and others; international directory of Focusing trainers; bulletin board of upcoming programs; articles on applications of Focusing in professional fields; books, audios, and DVDs about Focusing, and much more. The Focusing Institute is a membership organization with additional member benefits.

Books

Cornell, Ann Weiser. *The Power of Focusing: A Practical Guide to Emotional Self-Healing.* Oakland, Calif.: New Harbinger Publications, 1996. An excellent introductory text.

Gendlin, Eugene. *Focusing*. New York: Bantam Books, 2007. The classic introduction to Focusing and a gateway to Gendlin's many other fascinating books and articles.

Trungpa, Chögyam. *Shambhala: The Sacred Path of the Warrior*. Boston: Shambhala Publications, 2007. Another classic, with inspiring descriptions of the path of self-mastery, including chapters on synchronizing mind and body, overcoming habitual patterns, and authentic presence.

Index

About the Author

DAVID I. ROME is a teacher, writer, and consultant on applications of contemplative methods in personal, organizational, and social change. He is coeditor of *Mindfulness-Oriented Interventions for Trauma: Integrating Contemplative Practices* (Guilford Press, 2015). As managing director and senior fellow at the Garrison Institute from 2004 to 2011, he guided the development of programs on contemplative applications in K–12 education, trauma treatment, and climate change work. He was senior vice president for planning and development at Greyston Foundation, the pioneering Buddhist-inspired inner-city community development group, and president of Schocken Books in New York City.

David began practicing Buddhism in 1971 and served as private secretary to Tibetan contemplative master Chögyam Trungpa. He was closely involved in the early development of Naropa University and Shambhala International, and was a senior teacher of Shambhala Training. He studied Focusing with Eugene Gendlin, Ann Weiser Cornell, Robert Lee, and others. He is a Certifying Coordinator (senior trainer) with the Focusing Institute and conducts advanced training in meditation instruction for Shambhala International. His website is www.mindfulfocusing.com.